Never Enough

Never Enough

My Words Unfiltered

Pete Wicks

We know some topics can be hard to read. For anyone who would appreciate some advanced warning, this book contains mentions of struggles with mental health issues and attempted suicide.

First published in Great Britain in 2024 by Hodder Catalyst
An imprint of Hodder & Stoughton Limited
An Hachette UK company

1

Written with Arielle Steele

A CIP catalogue record for this title is available from the British Library

Hardback ISBN 9781399728393
ebook ISBN 9781399728416

Typeset in Electra by Hewer Text UK Ltd, Edinburgh
Printed and bound in Great Britain by Clays Ltd, Elcograf S.p.A.

Hodder & Stoughton policy is to use papers that are natural, renewable and recyclable products and made from wood grown in sustainable forests. The logging and manufacturing processes are expected to conform to the environmental regulations of the country of origin.

Hodder & Stoughton Limited
Carmelite House
50 Victoria Embankment
London EC4Y 0DZ

The authorised representative in the EEA is Hachette Ireland, 8 Castlecourt Centre, Castleknock Road, Castleknock, Dublin 15, D15 YF6A, Ireland

www.hoddercatalyst.co.uk

To Mum and Nan x

Contents

Contents

INTRODUCTION

Nowadays, I'm covered in tattoos – from my neck, more or less down to my feet. But, believe it or not, I was a blank canvas before the age of fifteen, when I decided it was time to get my first one. At that point, I already viewed myself as a proper geezer, and I had started going out to pubs and nightclubs. However, the bouncers occasionally clocked on to the fact I was just a kid, and they wouldn't let me in. I thought a tattoo would help me look older. In my mind, it meant more female attention and more beers. Happy days.

I didn't pre-plan it. I had no idea what I wanted the tattoo to be until I was inside the shop. I knew I wanted some kind of cursive writing (that was the big trend back then), and I thought it would be cool to get something in Latin. Not sure why I thought Latin was a good idea – I didn't know shit about it; I could barely speak English – but I didn't know what I wanted it to say. It was only when I was sitting in the waiting room that the phrase popped into my head: 'Never Enough'. And that has been etched into my forearm ever since (or, at least, I think that's what it says. I wouldn't know. I can't read Latin).

At the time, I didn't acknowledge why this weirdly depressing phrase felt so important or relevant. I was always the life and soul of the party – I wasn't some sort of emo moody kid – so it wasn't something I said a lot. But those words meant something to me, because I had never felt like I was ever enough. I still don't, to be perfectly honest with you.

I might seem confident, but these two simple words sum up the way I have felt my entire life. Back then, I never felt like I was enough for my parents. Later, I'd find myself with a 'more, more, more' attitude towards my career, partying and adrenaline-chasing, which meant I never felt satisfied. And now, I still feel all of that crap, but I'm also preoccupied with the fact I'm not doing enough to give back and make my time on this planet worth something. I have always tried to get better and be better in all aspects of my life, but I feel like I have always fallen short. I'm still carrying the words 'Never Enough' with me, both metaphorically and physically, because they're on my fucking arm. So, in a way, this book has been twenty years in the making.

That said, I didn't really want to write this, but as a nod to our podcast, you've got to do whatever you can to stay relevant in this world, right? I'm not sure why anyone would care what I have to say. However, I'm here now, and you've spent your hard-earned money on this book, so I'm going to try to make it worth-while – for both of us.

I have been in the public eye for the past decade, ever since I first appeared on the unscripted reality show *The Only Way Is Essex* (otherwise known as *TOWIE*). Since then, I've been doing all sorts of bits – from reality shows, to podcasting, to a thirst-trap calendar that outsold Justin Bieber (those were the days). Since I started out in this industry, people have held a lot of assumptions about me. The arrogant Lothario. The grumpy git. The bad boy. The stubborn dictator. The hairy, tattooed dickhead. To be honest, most of that is true. However, behind every identity or label, there's a lot more that makes a person. I've also done a fair bit of charity work, particularly with animals, so I'd hope that some of you know there's a nice person in there somewhere. But I also know that the caricature of Pete Wicks takes over, and the first impression probably isn't great. It's frustrating to feel misunderstood – we all want to be seen for who we really are. That doesn't just apply to 'celebrities' (God, I hate saying that word). Lots of us feel tied to certain identities and don't know how to escape them or how to ever grow out of them and move on. So I guess this book is partly my attempt to put the real, most vulnerable me on the table. Because if we can all understand ourselves better, we allow other people to understand us too.

The problem is, I think we all struggle to really know ourselves and each other. We're so used to judging other people based on shallow, surface-level characteristics – and then we compare ourselves against something that is completely manufactured. Yes, I blame social media for that. All you see, day in, day out, are pictures of perfect-looking people with perfect-looking lives. We all know that's not reality, but sometimes we need a bit of reminding. Behind every curated feed, there's someone with a fuck-ton of demons and struggles they're having to deal with. Just because someone is constantly posting from a beach in Dubai, doesn't mean they're happy with all they have.

They could be deeply lonely and unfulfilled. Just because someone is partying with their friends, doesn't mean they're not grieving the loss of someone they loved. I understand why we all want to show our best bits – it's human nature, ain't it? But I think it's important to show some of the harder shit too, because it reminds us we're not alone.

As a man, I feel an extra layer of responsibility to come clean about some of the shit I've been through, and still struggle with. I know fuck-all about history, but I can tell you for a fact that we've been living in a culture of toxic masculinity for centuries. *You have to be strong, you have to provide, you have to hold onto power. You can't cry, you can't show weakness, you can't seem 'feminine' in any way.* I know this is gradually changing, but we still have a way to go. Male addiction and suicide rates are shockingly high, and I believe a big reason for that is that many of us blokes still don't know how to process our emotions – because we've never been given permission to or we just have no outlet where it feels safe or comfortable to do so. It comes out in anger or aggression, or drowning our sorrows. I'm not on a high horse preaching about this – I'll be the first to admit that I'm one of these geezers – but, after losing the most important person in my life and reflecting a lot on where I've been and where I want to be, I know these attitudes aren't doing bits for me anymore. Let's face it – they're not working for any of us. Men, women, anyone. For the longest time, I've been suppressing a lot of my insecurities and traumas, and pretending they don't exist, but that just ain't cutting it anymore. We could all do with getting some stuff off our chests.

4

All of this to say: buckle up, because this book is going to get deep. When conversations get serious, my default is to take the piss or self-deprecate (and there will still be some of that, don't get me wrong – it is my book after all), but I think now is the right time to open up Pandora's box. We'll cover grief, where my fear of abandonment comes from, the most abusive trolling I've ever experienced and my use of unhealthy coping mechanisms like anger and booze. Don't worry, I promise this won't be the most miserable book you've ever read. I'll also take you behind the scenes of my life and this ridiculous industry I work in, and bring you in on all the wild nights and my dating life. I'll even lift the lid on my fake friendship with Samuel Thompson (I'm joking . . . or am I? You'll have to read on to find out).

I know my life is unique to me and me alone. Even after you've read a whole book about me, you still won't fully understand who I am. No two people are the same – and that's okay. My goal is just that some small part of my story resonates with you and makes you reflect on your own journey. Maybe, like me, you pay far too much attention to your flaws and this has a knock-on effect on your self-worth. Or, you feel a lot of pressure to live your life the 'right way' and you don't have a clue what that even is. Or, you feel like nothing you do is ever good enough to feel like you're worth something. I don't have all the answers for this shit, but I like to think I have some – even if I'm not the best at putting my own lessons into practice.

You should know that there will be hundreds of hypocrisies and contradictions in the pages ahead. But that's just life, ain't it? We're all complicated messes of human beings and life is full of shitty moments. The more we can lean into that, embrace it and fucking talk about it, the easier it will be to move forward and feel a bit more positive about all the good stuff. We might all be a bit messed up in our own ways, but there's still a lot of life to enjoy along the way. That's the plan, anyway.

A few words of warning before we get into it: I will be swearing – and if you don't like that, go fuck yourself. I may be drinking – the jury's still out on that one. I'll probably be crying as I delve into the depths of my soul. You won't have to see it, but you can visualise it if you want. You can read this book from start to finish or you can go to the chapters you think will be most helpful to you in a given moment. But this ain't a self-help book. I'm not here to tell you what to do or what you should take from reading this. You're an adult – you can make your own decisions. This is just my experience.

I know I said I never wanted to write this book, but you'll come to realise that some things I say are best taken with a pinch of salt. (A lot of the time, I say one thing and then I change my mind. Ain't nothing wrong with that – it's called growth, and we should all be open to it.) Teenage Pete never believed he would amount to anything and didn't think anyone would want to listen to anything he had to say, and he's now publishing a book about his life and his point of view. He never read any books, mind you, but he loved the sound of his own voice, so I'm sure he'd be over the moon. So, this is for that prick – and for every other person who feels like nothing they do is ever enough and they will never be just enough. Let's all go on this fucked-up adventure together.

CHAPTER 1

Don't Let Someone Else's
Death Be the Death of You

I know what you're thinking: 'Great, this grumpy fucker is start-ing his book in the most depressing way possible.' Yes, we're going to start by talking about death. Why? Because it took losing the most important person in my life for me to realise that I had to confront my demons head-on. It made me understand that there's a whole load of shit I'd been running away from, and that it was high time I faced it. Essentially, it's the whole reason I'm writing this fucking book in the first place. So where else to begin?

In May 2021, I lost my favourite person in the world – my nan. Look, I know that everyone loses grandparents; it's part of the cycle of life: you get old and then you die. I know that losing a grandparent isn't some kind of extraordinary occurrence. But it doesn't matter how old someone is when they die if they're your best friend. I know it sounds weird, but that's what my nan was to me. We could talk shit for hours and never get bored. She watched me go through some of my worst times and behave terribly, but, for some reason, she always thought I was special and worth something. She was my safety net and, without that,

I've had to find my own sense of safety. To be honest, it's been pretty fucking terrifying.

I tend not to talk about my nan and how much losing her has affected me because I don't think anyone cares, and there's no reason why they should. This isn't a fucking pity party, and I know I'm so fortunate to have the life that I have. But I want to tell you about who she was and how much I've struggled since she died – because we will all have the rug ripped out from underneath us at least once in our lives. You'll have your own losses and heartbreaks – the things you're trying to process or avoiding talking about; the things that make you drink too much, or behave erratically, or cry when nobody else is around. I'm sure you'll have your own version of my story. And I think that, maybe, it might help to know that you're not doing it wrong, and you're not alone.

For as long as I can remember, I've been obsessed with my nan. Generally, if I had to tell you about my childhood, I don't remember much. I grew up with my mum, dad and sister, moving between East London and Essex at various different points. My dad worked a lot and Mum stayed at home; they were very sociable and there were always tons of people in the house. Dad was competitive so I played on lots of sports teams – I played rugby and football, I swam and I ran. I was the captain of everything. It was all pretty wholesome and nice, really – just what you want your childhood to be. That is, until my dad left when I was eleven years old, and everything went a bit off the rails from there (but we'll get into that later).

Even though everything else is a bit of a blur, the one thing that stands out is my nan. In fact, my earliest memory was giving her the nickname Nanny Toe. I called her that because, when I first started speaking as a toddler, she had an ingrown toenail and wouldn't stop going on about it. 'This fucking toe's doing my head in!' I can remember her saying – and so she became Nanny Toe.

She was my mum's mum, and she lived in Dagenham when I was growing up – so not too far away from our house. She was a proper old East End battleaxe – and I mean that in the nicest way. She'd been through a lot; she didn't have the best upbringing, and my mum's dad left when his kids were very young, leaving Nan to hold everything together. It's hard to pinpoint why she was so special, but, as I've gotten older, I've realised that it's her presence. Some people just have it – where, for some reason, you feel so comfortable and safe around them. Some people just have a gift for being there for people – and that was Nan. She viewed herself as a kind of spiritual healer and ended up being that person in her neighbourhood who everyone went to for advice. I remember going round to her house and I'd have to make tea for all these ex-cons who would come to see her; all these big geezers who you wouldn't expect to be sat with this old dear. But it made sense, because she was so forgiving and empathetic. She was the most compassionate person I've ever met. She believed that, whether you've done wrong or fucked up, everyone has an opportunity to put that right and have some sort of redemption. She always saw the best in people, even when some people don't have the best in them.

But, to me, she was also just Nanny Toe. I can still picture her so vividly. She was ginger, but she insisted she was 'strawberry blonde'; her hair was always curled, and she always had a ridiculous tan, like a Peperami in a fucking wig. She was constantly covered in shit jewellery – she wore a big gold cross around her neck, and cheap rings all over her fingers. She always smelled like cheap perfume. Her husband (who I called my granddad) was a bus conductor and they didn't have a lot of money, but they'd save up everything they had for adventures to Sri Lanka, Barbados and Jamaica. Afterwards, we'd have to sit through pictures of her getting pissed on the beach. She was the life and soul of every party – always singing and dancing. She smoked constantly, probably about forty a day. Come to think of it, I probably get a lot of who I am from her.

Rather than spending school holidays with my mates, I'd spend most of my time at my nan's. We'd play cards for hours on end, and I'd try to help her around the house – repainting her walls, but getting more paint on the carpet than the fucking walls, or going off to B&Q to buy bamboo poles for her garden. She was always fucking about in her little garden – she loved it. Even when I was really young, we would bicker and take the piss out of each other. Once, she took me to McDonald's, ordered a Filet-O-Fish, and then asked for a knife and fork. I was like, 'you're so fucking embarrassing' and stormed off. She found it hilarious. The reality was that I wasn't embarrassed of her; I was embarrassed that my best mate was an old lady. I think it probably seemed strange to a lot of people, but I've always felt older than my age, and I think she always seemed younger, so we met in the middle. Whenever we shouted at each other, it was always completely unserious. She would call me a fucking prick and I'd call her an old witch. It was quite an odd dynamic for anyone who walked past us in the street. But that was just what we were like.

I basically wanted to go everywhere with her. There was one occasion, just after my parents split up, when we went on holiday to Portugal, and Nan and my granddad came too. I would've been about eleven years old. One day, they wanted to get some peace and quiet, so they walked about forty minutes to the nearby town to go to a cafe and have some alone time. When I realised that Nan wasn't coming to spend the day with us, I thought, 'Bollocks, why hasn't she taken me?' So I walked on my own into town, wandered around and somehow managed to find her, sitting outside a restaurant smoking a fag. She was like, 'What are you doing here? You've got a fucking radar for me!' Bear in mind, this was before mobile phones, so my mum was scared shitless wondering where I'd gone. But I just liked to follow Nan around. My mum would call me her little fucking shadow.

We loved to wind each other up. There was one occasion, when I was a teenager, and she was staying over downstairs. I was awake at around 3am, and I could hear that she was getting out of bed to use the bathroom. I thought it would be really funny to wait at the bottom of the stairs for her to come around the corner so I could scare her. So I waited there until she came past, and then I switched on the light and shouted 'RAAH'. But it was me who got the fright of my life – she was stark bollock naked. 'What the fuck are you doing, you little shit!' she screamed. That's not what you want to see, I can tell you. It was fucking horrendous.

On another occasion, she was staying with me for the week while my mum was away. I must've been about thirteen. I had been round at a pal's house and got into a fight, so the police dropped me home. When she closed the door, she screamed at me for about fifteen minutes straight – effing and blinding about my behaviour – before making me a cup of tea (she was always drinking tea), taking a drag of her cigarette and calmly saying, 'Well, we won't tell your mother. Just don't do it again.' She then used it to blackmail me for the rest of the week. 'Clean the whole house otherwise I'll tell your mother you were in trouble with the police,' she'd say. I basically had to do whatever she wanted. But I didn't really mind. In the end, she always kept my secrets and I always kept hers.

When I was around sixteen years old, she and my granddad moved to Alicante in Spain for a few years. It had always been her dream to live in the sun, so she moved there to retire. I hated it. During that time, I was a bit all over the shop mentally, and I attribute that to not having her around as much to ground me. I would go out and visit her a fair bit, and she'd come back, but it was hard. It was when she was out there that she started getting sick. Her heart was playing up and she was getting physically weaker. Because I didn't see her as often, the deterioration was noticeable. She was still as quick-witted as she always was, but it was visibly quite a shock. I used to force her to play football with me, and now here she was struggling to get up and down stairs. It was the first time I realised that she wasn't invincible.

After a few years, Mum and I decided that she needed to be nearer to us so we could help look after her. By that time, I was in my early twenties and had done alright for myself in the City. So I moved back to Essex from London and bought Nan a flat that was really close to my mum. We were all within walking distance of each other, and I was so happy to have her back. I was a fully-grown man by this point, with my own life and responsibilities, but if I couldn't sleep at 3am, I'd call her. She always seemed to be able to sense when I needed her. She'd say, 'I was already awake – I knew you was gonna call. I had a feeling.' She struggled to sleep too, so sometimes we'd chat on the phone for an hour (once she'd worked out how to use a mobile), or I'd go round to hers and we'd sit up playing cards. I don't even know what we'd talk about, but we could chat away for hours.

For some reason, Nan always thought there was something special about me. She'd say 'you belong on the fucking screen', and I would just laugh it off. So, of course, she was in her element when I started on *TOWIE*. She had pictures of me all over her house and, when nurses would go round to check on her, they'd ask, 'Oh, are you a fan of Pete Wicks?' And she'd proudly reply, 'He's my grandson.' She even asked my mum to print off pictures of me to sign so she could hand out fucking autographs (even though obviously no one wanted them). She'd watch every episode, and would always tell me if I was being a knob-head and needed to apologise to someone. I'd do whatever she told me to do because I trusted her more than I trusted myself.

She also loved looking after my dogs, Eric and Peggy, when I wasn't around. I think it's because she needed to be looked after, so she enjoyed being able to look after something. It made her feel useful. That said, she wasn't the best at taking care of them. I'd go round to pick them up and be like, 'Why the fuck is Eric frothing at the mouth?' And she'd say she gave him Refreshers sweets. I'd be fuming, and she'd say, 'Well, you used to like Refreshers.' And I'd say, 'Well, I'm not a fucking dog!' Still, they survived it – and they loved her.

In the end, Nan was sick for about seven years before she passed. She never wanted to go into a home because she hated the idea of not being able to look after herself. But when my granddad died, she needed extra care. There was one time she fell over and stayed on the floor for three hours because she couldn't get back up. There was another time when she called me in the middle of the night saying she didn't feel well, but she refused to let me call an ambulance and insisted I come to pick her up. At that time, I had a Porsche 911, which is very low, and I had to carry her into the car. When we got to A&E, the bloody car was so low I basically had to manhandle her to get her out. I can't imagine how it must've looked for all the people in A&E watching me dragging an eighty-year-old woman out of a sports car with her yelling, 'You're fucking hurting me, you prick!' She never wanted to be a burden, and I understand that I was one of the few people she was willing to be vulnerable with.

Eventually, we all had to accept that she needed extra help, so we moved her into a nursing home. They told us she wasn't allowed to smoke there, so she got me to smuggle in 100 Mayfair Blues in a perfume gift box. And that same day, I got a call to say she'd set off the smoke alarm in the whole home. They knew they wouldn't be able to stop her smoking (she did what the fuck she wanted), so they ended up moving her to a downstairs room so she could have a cigarette out of the French doors. She moved there around the time Covid happened, which was fucking horrendous because she was suddenly on her own after spending so much of her life surrounded by people. It made me angry speaking to her sometimes because she'd have real down days where she'd say she didn't want to be in the world anymore. It would get me riled up because I didn't ever want her to think that. I didn't ever want her to leave me. I know now that reacting like this was selfish of me. She'd been the one who had spent her whole life fixing people, supporting people who needed it. And now here she was saying she was the one in pain, and I batted her feelings away. I just didn't want to imagine life without her. Now, I regret not giving her the space to express that. She was allowed to feel shit, but I just hated the thought of it more than anything.

She spent her last three weeks in hospital. Me and mum visited her in shifts: one of us would do the morning and one the evening. She did have other family and friends, but us three were the closest, and we wanted to make sure she never felt lonely. There were points when she seemed so ill that I thought she might go, but then she'd suddenly turn a corner, and she'd be moaning about the hospital food or demanding ice cream, which was all she felt like eating. I'd sit and hold her hand, and we'd talk – although she wasn't making a lot of sense by that point. But every so often, we'd have a five-minute conversation that just made complete sense. Despite everything, she was my Nan, right until the end.

The day she died, I had been in London seeing friends. Mum called me and told me I needed to get to the hospital quickly. Nan didn't want to do it anymore – she was in too much pain and was going to ask the doctors to turn off her oxygen machine. After so long insisting to her, and myself, that she could get better, I finally needed to come to terms with her life ending. But wow, it was the hardest fucking thing I've ever done. Mum and I sat either side of her, holding each hand. I can remember the last words she said to me as if it were yesterday: 'You're my soulmate.'

A lot clicked for me at that point. Often, when people talk about 'soulmates', you think about romantic love, but it doesn't always have to be. Of course, she was my nan, so she didn't have a fucking choice to be part of my life, but I do believe she was meant to be part of it. And I was meant to be part of hers. I don't know what's out there, and I don't necessarily believe in God. I don't know about any of that stuff. But Nan always believed there was something bigger, so I would never write it off. And I certainly think there are times when you have a connection with someone and, for some reason, it's a stronger connection than what you have with other people. That could be a friend or a relative. It could be someone you've known your whole life or someone you just click with as soon as you meet them in adulthood. Whether that's because of some higher power, I don't know. But having a person like that is amazing and rare. And losing them will fucking break your heart. As Nan drifted off, I just kept saying, 'I'm sorry.' I'm not really sure why, but I think it was because she was such a magical person and she deserved better than investing all her magic in me.

There was something about her that understood me before I even understood myself. I will always remember the time she said she wanted to come with me to get a tattoo. I got covered in tattoos fairly young – I was still a teenager – and I told my nan, who was about seventy at the time, that I was going off to have some more work done on my arm. I think she was over visiting from Spain. 'Can I come?' she asked. I said that of course she could, and asked her why. She said she just wanted to see what it was like. 'She'll fucking end up getting one,' my mum joked, and we laughed – but then we got in the car and Nan turned to me and went, 'I want one.' I said, 'You're fucking joking.' I think maybe she was joking, but then I said, 'Go on, I fucking dare you,' and so I think she wanted to prove to me that she could. So after she sat and watched me have mine done, she told the tattoo artist that she wanted to get one too – 'It's got to be to do with you,' she said, looking at me. In the end, she decided on a little P inside a star. She got the star because she said I was destined to be a star. Obviously, I wouldn't go as far as to say I'm a fucking 'star', but this was five years before I ended up on TV, and it's weird that she always had a feeling that I'd end up doing something like that. 'You have a gift for being able to impact people's lives in a good way,' she'd say, 'but you hide from it.'

Anyway, she got the tattoo on her ankle because it was the only bit of skin that wasn't folded over. I held her hand while she had it done and she cried because it was so painful. The ankle can be pretty fucking nippy so I'm not surprised. But she was so happy with it. I remember her showing my mum and Mum saying, 'What the fuck have you done, you look like a right slapper,' and her going, 'Oh fuck off Tracy.' It was just such a special, yet strange, experience.

But the thing that stands out most to me is, when we were in the car on the way home, Nan turned to me and said, 'Why do you like getting tattoos so much?' People ask me this a lot, and it's difficult to answer because I'm not particularly creative, and a lot of my tattoos don't necessarily mean anything. But I suppose I quite like the pain of it. There's something satisfying about it. I told her this and shrugged. 'You find comfort in pain,' she responded. 'You need to start finding comfort in happiness.'

I brushed her off at the time, but those words have stuck with me, and they've tortured me quite a lot since she died. In the years she was sick, I know she was worried about me. 'I'm hanging on until you're happy,' she had said. And I didn't really manage to get my shit together before she died. It's one of my biggest regrets.

I'm not exactly sure why I wasn't happy. I had almost all the things you could want in life: a fun job, money, great mates, loads of opportunities and privileges. I always appeared happy on the outside, but my nan knew that something on the inside of me was broken. Nan could see through the mask I put out to the world, and how I hid my pain behind tattoos and parties and chasing adrenaline. When you lose the person who understands you so completely, it can feel like you've lost your anchor to who you are.

In the first few weeks after she died, the shock and grief were overwhelming. But I channelled all my energy into being there for my mum. My mum is a fucking angel – I love her more than anything – and I've always been protective of her. I don't know whether it's a male thing (or my lack of a father figure from the age of eleven onwards), but I've always felt like I have to be the strong one, especially when it comes to my family. I've always wanted to be the one people can rely on. So I just did all I could to make sure she was alright. But really my idea of 'strength' just meant suppressing my emotions. I can admit that I find it easier to take on someone else's pain, because it's a distraction from my own. Often, the person people turn to for advice is struggling the most deep down. I knew for a fact I would be there when anyone else needed me, so why couldn't I be there for myself? Really, the idea of being 'strong' is just an illusion; just another mask we put on so that we don't risk exposing all our messiness to the world. My nan could see through a lot of the bollocks in people. She knew I wasn't as strong as I made out to be, and I'm now in the process of accepting that.

Her funeral was on the hottest day of the year. There were people there from all over the world; people she had helped who had been in prison, people who hadn't seen me since I was a little kid. She was two hours late to her own fucking funeral because there was traffic on the M11, and everyone was sweating their tits off. When I got up to speak, I said, 'She'll be fucking laughing at us, as she's not the only one being cremated today.' Of course, I had to start with some humour – she wouldn't have had it any other way. And then I read a letter I had written to her, and that was fucking hard to get through, let me tell you.

Afterwards, I went into action mode. We had her wake in a pub and I just tried to make sure everyone was alright. At the end of the evening, I went back to my mum's and put her to bed, and then I walked home. I was that drunk that I didn't even know how I got home. The next morning, my suit was ripped and I was covered in bruises. I think I fell down a ditch or something. Who knows what I fucking did.

In 2022, I tried to carry on and throw myself into work, but then I'd shut myself away and feel a tsunami of pain when I was on my own. I didn't know what to do. I was very angry. I drank a lot. I didn't treat myself particularly well. I had never felt so alone, so I surrounded myself with people as much as I could. I basically flipped between looking after people, distraction and self-destruction. I'm not saying that's the best way to grieve, but I think it's a realistic process that a lot of us go through. Grief is so complex, so of course we're going to react in complex (and often unhealthy) ways. It's easy to beat yourself up for not doing grief 'right'. Of course, it's important not to hurt other people in the process, but I think there's no wrong or right when it comes to grief. You have to just do what you need to do to prevent yourself from falling into a pit of despair. It's kind of just about surviving, at least in the immediate aftermath. The real work comes later.

I'm really lucky that I have loads of supportive friends, but, as time went on, the support started to wane. I don't blame people for checking in less – it's natural. The world keeps on turning, and life gets back to normal. I think it's at this point – around six months to a year – when a different wave of grief sets in. This time can feel even lonelier because there's an expectation that you should be 'over it', whatever that means. I think this is the time when you really have to confront what the world is going to look like without that person, and what your place is in that world. I was still being kept awake at night with the memories of Nan's final moments, when she looked so weak and in pain. It was traumatising, to be fucking honest with you. The worst part was I knew she was the only person who could make me feel better, and she wasn't there to help. And then, I'd go into a spiral of feeling selfish and angry at myself for making it all about me. It's a natural reaction, though, and I'm trying to forgive myself for feeling that way.

For a long time, it was my nan who kept me balanced. I think it was the fact that she had never let me down, when so many other people did, and that made me feel safe and protected. Without that balance, I felt like I was falling off the edge. Losing someone can be the catalyst for realising that you're ultimately on your own in this life. That might sound fucking depressing, but it's really only as negative as you make it. You can't rely on another person to be your safety net – whether that's a parent or a partner or whoever – because they won't be around forever. You have to create your own safety net ... and a lot of that comes from building your self-worth. I'm not saying I've achieved that. Far from it. I told you this ain't a self-help book. But I am saying that I'm willing to look for those answers, to try to build a more robust net for myself, to mimic the one my nan had made for me. It's hard, but you have to give it a go.

I'm writing this chapter almost two years on from the death of my nan, and I feel embarrassed that I still haven't moved on yet.

To be honest, I'm making peace with the fact I will never move on. I don't believe any of that 'time's a healer' crap. I'm not sure you ever get over the things that leave their marks on you; you simply learn to live with them. You can't reverse what has happened, but you have to come to terms with it – whether that's losing a person, or a big breakup, or whatever horrible event that you have nightmares about. But, you know what? That's okay. You don't have to move on. You don't have to forget. But you do have to keep finding reasons to keep pushing forward.

When it comes to grief specifically, it's hard to give any one-size-fits-all advice because everyone's experience with grief is so individual. A lot of the time, when I tell people how I feel, they say they understand because they lost their nan too, or whoever else. But they'll never understand. Not really. Just like I will never understand their grief. You'll have your own set of experiences, and your own relationship with that person that no one else can really make sense of. That's also a good thing, though, because you have your own unique set of memories with that person that no one can take away. Being alone in something isn't always something to feel sad about. My nan always believed that we are all so individual and special – this can be a burden, but it's also a superpower.

I definitely didn't grieve in the healthiest ways, but I would never judge someone for how they choose to manage. I think you should process the pain however the fuck you want to. When I eventually moved past the destruction phase, though, I found it helpful to think about what my nan's life meant and how I could carry that on into my own life. I thought that the way she felt about me was an opportunity to make her proud. I thought that, maybe, she's somewhere else right now and she's watching over me – and I don't want to disappoint her. Like I said, I don't know if I believe in all that. I'm not religious. But if thinking about some kind of afterlife and greater purpose makes mourning easier, there's nothing wrong with telling yourself that. Choose to believe something that will comfort you. Why not?

Someone once told me that losing someone allows you to become a tribute to their memory. So, now I try to think about everything my nan was and try to embody that in my own life. I can be a judgemental fucker, but she always saw the best in people, so I'm trying to see the world through her eyes. She was always the shoulder to cry on, so I'm trying to be that for the people I love too. She was always the life and soul of the party and, well, I don't need much encouragement to drink and smoke, but I sometimes need reminding to enjoy every moment. All my nan wanted was for me to be happy – and, if she's watching, I want her to see me that way. If you've lost someone, I recommend you do the same. Think about all their best qualities and then work out how they can live on through you. Of course, nothing you do can ever replace that person. You'll probably never be as fucking amazing as they were (sorry), but you can take small steps to try.

You might be reading this in the early stages of grief, where everything feels so dark and heavy, and like it'll last forever. I've been there. I know I've said you'll never move on, but the good news is that you will start to find moments of beauty in life again. One day, you'll notice that your distraction tactics are actually working at distracting you, and you'll laugh with a group of friends, and you'll feel the sun on your skin, and you'll think, 'This is actually a really fucking nice day.'

I knew that things would be alright when I started noticing the kindness of strangers again. Like, one particular time that an old lady stopped me in the street in London. She had the happiest face I've ever seen in my life. She said: 'Excuse me, but I just had to tell you that you have the most beautiful eyes I've ever seen.' I was really startled, and said, 'Thank you.' Then she said, 'But there's sadness in your eyes, and you shouldn't be sad because time runs out.' I have thought about this moment so many times since then and it gave me a weird feeling of comfort. Maybe it was a sign from my nan or maybe it was a load of bollocks. But it was a small, fleeting interaction that reminded me that the world isn't so fucked up after all.

The truth is, life ain't a fairy tale. It's mostly shit. But there are glimmers of light among all the shit. My biggest glimmer of light was my nan – but it's not like she took all the light with her. I know it sounds cliché, but you really just have to look for it. You need to have hope that good things will come. You have to keep moving forward. You can't let someone else's death be the death of your own life. Otherwise, what's the fucking point?

I'm on that journey with you. I want to really, fully live – not just exist. I want to be better. I want to be happy. I know I am extremely blessed and lucky to have spent thirty-three years of my life with my nan, and I'm not going to let the love she poured into me go to waste. Loss is the worst thing any of us can go through, but grief is also a privilege. Because it shows we had someone so fucking special to begin with – and not everyone is so lucky. My nan dealt with far more shit than I ever have, and yet I watched her wake up every day with emotional intelligence, compassion and lust for life. She took the bad in life and spun it into something good. I want to live like she did. If I could be even half the person she was, I'd be very happy. So, let's all make sure we honour the people we have loved and lost, and try our best to find our own reasons for living. Just because someone who unconditionally loved you has gone, doesn't mean that you're not still worthy of love. I know it's not fucking easy to believe that, but you can keep coming back to this page to remind yourself.

Final Fucking Thoughts: Don't let someone else's death be the death of you

★ Time doesn't heal your pain, but it does make it easier to live with.

★ If you've lost someone you love, try to find ways to make their best qualities live through you. If they were generous, be generous. If they were funny, be funny (or at least try). You can keep people with you, even when they're gone.

★ Don't let anyone judge you for how you deal with grief. You had your own relationship with that person, so it's your own journey through loss – no one else's.

CHAPTER 2

Listen to What Your Anger Is Telling You

If you've watched any shows that I've been in or listened to my podcast, you might assume that I'm quite an angry person. And yes, you would be right. Almost anything can grind my gears and get me all riled up. Here's an incomplete list of things that make me angry, in no particular order:

★ Hearing people being rude to waiters or acting like people are beneath them.

★ The smell of Febreze in an Uber when I'm hungover.

★ A badly poured pint of Guinness.

★ Voice notes. Give me the bullet points – I don't need your fucking life story.

★ London traffic.

★ Waiting fucking ages for my new shoes to arrive.

★ People cancelling. If you say you're going to do it, fucking do it.

★ When someone messages you, you don't reply and then they message you with something else or send a question mark. Fuck off.

★ Pretty much everything about people. I despise people. Real happy guy.

. . . I could go on and on.

I don't necessarily think it's a bad thing to feel angry. It's a normal human emotion, and it's unsurprising we feel it a lot given we live in a shit world full of shit people. There are plenty of reasons to be angry, and I don't think we should pretend life is all rainbows and butterflies and that nothing pisses us off. However, anger becomes a big problem when it comes out in destructive ways – both to yourself and other people. I know, because I've been there. In the past, I've struggled to regulate my anger and it has come out in fits of rage that have ended up hurting other people (sometimes in physical fights when I was a teenager), my surroundings and – most often – myself.

Anger is a bit of a dirty word that a lot of us don't want to talk about. Probably because it's associated with violence. Many of us don't want to admit we have a problem with our anger because we worry it means there's something fundamentally wrong with us and we're bad people. But I think men, especially, need to face our anger head-on. And I say men because studies have shown that more of us struggle with anger issues than women do. It's not that women don't feel anger as much, it's just that (I believe) men don't really know what to do with all our other emotions, so anger is just the way they present themselves. Sadness, resentment, fear and anxiety . . . they can all show up looking like anger. And I think if we can get to the bottom of the real reasons why we lose it over the most insignificant things, then we can control our anger, rather than letting it control us.

✳   ✳   ✳

I wasn't always an angry person. I was a pretty happy kid – really independent and sociable. My mum says I didn't really throw tantrums and I was happy as Larry wherever she took me. I was a little fucking angel, actually. It was only when I was a teenager that I became a real dickhead – and I guess not that much has changed since then.

If I had to pinpoint where my anger began, I'd say it was around the time my parents split up. Before that, my main goal in life was to make my dad proud. I've already mentioned I played every sport in the book, and my dad loved that. He'd always come and watch my matches or races, and he'd tell me what I did well and also what I needed to improve on. His criticisms weren't particularly mean, but they made me want to be better. I was so keen to impress him. If I won something or played really well, he'd say he was proud of me, and that meant the absolute world.

I think it meant so much to me because he wasn't the kind of person to show a lot of emotion. I think lots of people grow up with the same dynamic – where your mum is proper mumsy and warm, and your dad is just a bit cold. I guess it's a generational thing. It was all stiff upper lip, you don't moan when things go wrong, you just dust yourself off and crack on. Dad didn't show a lot of emotion and I think I absorbed that, believing that's what a man does. You hold it together.

My parents met when they were very young. My mum moved to London when she was sixteen to work and met my dad there, who was two years older. I know they loved each other at first, but it wasn't always easy. My mum had to do a lot. She stopped working to be a housewife when my dad got back out to work, and she had to give up so much of her life for that marriage. I'm not saying it was his fault – he provided really well for her, and he was struggling in his own ways – but I think it must've been hard for my mum holding everything together when my dad wasn't necessarily all there emotionally.

It turned out that my parents hadn't been happy for a while. But, to be honest with you, I never really saw anything. I think there was more that went on behind the scenes that I wasn't aware of. It didn't feel like an unhappy household – I think they did what they could to keep things normal. In the end, when it eventually fell apart, my mum had been having an affair with a man called Tony, who she's still with now. She met him because I played rugby with his son. I think I've blocked out a lot of my memories from this time so I'm not exactly sure how I found out – whether she told me directly or it became obvious over time when we were spending more and more time with him. But I know Mum and Tony were both going through rough times in their marriages and that's how they got close. And one day, my parents sat us down on the sofa to say they were getting divorced.

Again, I don't really remember what happened next. But I knew we were selling the house and we moved to another place with my mum, and Tony was there a lot. I had a lot of resentment towards him at the time, and I think partly I blamed myself for them meeting, so I acted like a little shit towards him. I'm not proud of that, but I just wanted my dad. I wanted to go and live with him instead, but he didn't want me. At least, that's the way I saw it. I know it was a lot more complicated than that, and it wasn't really anything to do with me, but when you're a kid that kind of shit can make you feel like you're not wanted.

There was one time, at some point when all this upheaval was happening, that I went for a walk with my dad around the fields near our house, and it was the first time I'd ever seen him cry. He completely broke down and was talking about how he wanted to end it all. I remember thinking, 'What the fuck is going on?' It was so alien to me, suddenly viewing my parents as real people with their own shit and struggles, and especially seeing my dad so emotional. But he told me to never say a word about it and we never spoke about it again. Like a lot of boys, I was taught that it's better to keep your emotions inside, and you should feel ashamed if you ever let your guard down like that.

At first, Dad moved to the other side of London – about an hour and a half away – so I saw him on occasional weekends. I hated going to see him; it felt awkward and weird, like we were being forced to see each other, rather than how natural and seamless it was when we lived together and he would just show up at my games to cheer me on. Having said that, there was one occasion that I did really enjoy. Dad had always want-ed to learn to scuba-dive, which meant that I wanted to learn to scuba-dive too, so, when I was about thirteen, he took me to learn how to dive in a quarry in Leicester. It was probably the worst place in the world to learn to dive – it was fucking freezing – but it was so fun doing it together. After that, we went on holiday to Sharm el-Sheikh in Egypt to dive there, and it was amazing. It was probably the closest I had been to him, spending a solid week together, just the two of us, and exploring amazing shipwrecks and coral reefs. I thought maybe this was what our relationship would turn into – lots of adventures and one-on-one bonding time. Maybe the split wouldn't be so bad after all.

But that was that. It never happened again, and we saw each other less and less. Eventually, he decided there wasn't much left for him in the UK so he moved to the Middle East, and I only visited him a couple of times. Our relationship went back to feeling forced and awkward, and eventually we became estranged. Looking back, I don't blame him for fucking off. I think he was struggling with everything that happened a lot more than he let on. But, at the time, I just thought: clearly I'm not enough for him to want to stay.

This was all happening at the same time as I was starting secondary school, which is already a pretty monumental life change. It felt like a big jump, going from primary to secondary school. And I'm sure going through puberty and being full of testosterone didn't help things. My nan was the only person I could talk to about what I was going through, but, even then, I didn't want to be a burden to her. So I shut up shop and learned to bottle it all up. But the thing is, when you bottle up emotions, they don't just disappear – they end up bursting out in other ways. And, for me, that was rage.

For the first couple of years, I was quieter than normal – not my usual cheeky, independent self. But then all my anger would come out in explosions in my bedroom and I'd punch whatever was in front of me. My mum was constantly having to replaster the walls from where I'd put my fist through them. I carried on playing sports, but I was always being sent to the bench for getting into fights. I was the smallest kid on the football pitch running around like a fucking thug, with a shaved head calling everyone a c*nt, like a little fucking Jason Statham. I have a really vivid memory of an under-fourteens rugby match, where my mum came to watch. I got into a fight on the pitch and another parent was shouting at me, calling me an animal. My mum was so embarrassed and called me a fucking idiot, and I don't blame her.

I would go out of my way to rile people up and get on their nerves. When I started working at a local hotel as a teenager, glass-collecting and whatnot, I ended up hanging around with a lot of older kids. I was the youngest in the group and often the smallest, so I'd yap away like a fucking terrier at their knees to aggravate them until they snapped and I'd have an excuse to fly off the handle and get into a physical fight.

If I saw people behaving badly, that was an excuse too. There was one time, I was around a group of acquaintances and I noticed this one geezer taking the piss out of someone who was quiet and shy. I really hate a bully, me. So I verbally gave them some shit – I was like, 'Shut the fuck up,' and was probably being a bit threatening to tell the truth. I knew I was testing him in front of people, and it was a show of dominance. I never wanted to be fucking fronted. I can't remember exactly what happened next, but I know I punched him and then he smashed a piece of wood across my forehead (who knows where he got it from). I won't tell you what I did back, but let's just say it wasn't a good night all in. I still have a scar above my eyebrow from that fucking plank of wood.

I know a lot of sane people would think, 'Why the fuck did you do that?' I would go out of my way to put myself into these stupid fucking situations. But if you relate to being an angry person, then you'll know that there's a rush that's difficult to explain. It's like a surge of adrenaline, when you release all of the shit you've been storing inside. It was rarely about whatever fucking thing I was losing it over, and more about needing to let it all out. Anything would set me off – I'd go from 0 to 100 faster than you can say 'Pirate Pete'. I had absolutely no patience. If I lost my keys or was given a shitty shift at the hotel, I'd go into some kind of frenzy and tear my room to pieces. I knew it wasn't healthy, but I knew that every explosion was normally followed by a brief period of calm and clarity. In the moments after an outburst, I'd feel like a weight had been lifted. My life became a cycle of explode-calm, explode-calm, explode-calm.

But the serenity never lasted long because then I'd look around at the damage and think, 'What the fuck am I doing?' Then the shame and guilt would come. You feel guilty for other people having to be around you when you're like that, and shame for being unable to control yourself or deal with your emotions in a way that is constructive or beneficial. I hated it when people I loved had to see me angry like that, but it felt like the only way I could process things. And it's happened quite a few times over the years where my outbursts have pushed people away. I've always known it's not necessarily healthy, but it was just part of how I dealt with things.

Hindsight is a beautiful thing, and I can now see clear as day why I lashed out all the time. My purpose as a kid had always been to make my dad proud and, with him living abroad and not really wanting to see me, I didn't know how to do that anymore. No amount of awards or trophies seemed to impress him anymore and, without his attention, I didn't know what the point in me was. Then there's the fact my mum was struggling with her own mental health problems (which we'll come back to later). It was fucking painful seeing her so low and I felt like I wasn't enough to help her. Nothing I did could fix all the shit that was broken. I couldn't make anything better. I think that's why, now, I tend to take on everyone else's shit and try to help them solve it. I fucking hate the feeling of being useless and not having a purpose. And so, I think those overwhelming feelings of uselessness made me angry at the world and angry at myself.

I hesitate to say that it was trauma from my childhood that made me like this. I wouldn't describe my childhood as traumatic – it wasn't horrendous all the time and this ain't a fucking pity party. I know I'm really lucky to have been raised how I was, going to a million different sports every weekend and having family (especially my nan) who I could lean on. I was always taken care of. But, yeah, I guess some of the things that happened between the ages of ten and fifteen did shape the way I am today. I thought I didn't fucking need anyone, and I was so self-reliant, but it's only now, twenty years later, that I can look back and go – actually, I wasn't fine. And I think the one thing I needed was the last thing I wanted . . . comfort.

See, there's a big difference between 'want' and 'need'. Your conscious mind tells you what you want and don't want – for me, I didn't want to be around people, I didn't want to be a burden on anyone. But in my subconscious brain, I really fucking needed that love and support. I didn't want to cause people shit. I didn't want to be more of a reason why people didn't want to stick around, and I didn't want to be a fucking failure. So, instead, I self-destructed. Anger naturally pushes people away. People get scared when you're angry. And I think I knew that, deep down, because I didn't want people to get too close. And I think I'm still like that to this day – letting someone in, and allowing them to see my vulnerable side, scares the shit out of me. (In fact, writing all of this now scares the shit out of me, but here we are.)

Anyway, I know that people have dealt with far worse than I ever have, but I'm getting comfortable with admitting that some things did fuck me up. I think a lot of us (men, especially) have this tendency to say, 'Nothing has affected me, I'm too strong to have experienced trauma.' We think it's weak. But this is a big barrier to moving forward. It can help to admit that maybe you were traumatised somewhere along the way. Just because something is common (like parents splitting up) doesn't mean it can't be traumatising. Everyone reacts differently to the events that happen to them. What causes trauma for you might not have affected me in the slightest, and vice versa. I think acknowledging the pain in your past is a first step towards working out why you are the way you are. And just because you're acknowledging why you are the way you are, doesn't mean you can blame your past for your actions. Those struggles might be the catalyst for my anger, but I also take full responsibility for the times I have lashed out. Digging into your past isn't about finding something or someone else to blame things on. It's about understanding yourself better so that you can make changes.

The first time I admitted to myself that my anger was a problem was about five years before my nan died. We went to the funeral of one of our relatives and there was another relative there who I didn't get on with, to say the least. I saw that person at the funeral and it just set me off – I was full of fucking rage, squaring up to him while everyone told me to calm down. I ended up leaving early because I felt like I could've killed him, I was that angry. I had generally always been really calm around my nan – she made me feel calm – and it was the first time she had seen me like that, and she wasn't able to help. It really upset her. It's painful to think about it now, actually, how upset she was. It was a fucking funeral too – I shouldn't have been thinking of me. It was really selfish and I was unable to get a handle on it. Nan wasn't well at the time either. I know she was really worried about me. That's when I thought: 'Shit. This is actually not okay.'

It's interesting that we think of anger as a show of strength and dominance, when actually it's anything but. When you scream at someone or break a fucking glass, you think you're asserting yourself. But you actually look like a mug. You feel like you're in control, but you quickly realise that's an illusion and you couldn't be less in control. Afterwards, you feel weak because you know that it was weakness that caused such a destructive reaction.

I think we've got our ideas about what is 'strong' and what is 'weak' all back to front. We tend to think of crying and breaking down as weak, but actually that's just another way of letting out your emotions, and it's much less destructive. I'm generalising here, but I think when women get upset they're more likely to let their emotions out and talk about it, and men are more likely to just get so angry they can't even think clearly, let alone talk about it, or go completely silent. We've been taught that weeping is embarrassing or pathetic, so getting angry is like a show of masculinity. It's like: 'You get angry now and then? Okay, that's what men do – but we don't fucking cry.'

That's bullshit. I think women are much more emotionally intelligent than men – they know that it's a healthier way to process shit if you cry and talk to people. You let it out, and you're not being a fucking hurricane in the process. I don't think it's our fault that we're so bad at processing emotions; it's just the way we were raised and socialised differently. I think we have been trained to distance ourselves from our feelings. Generally speaking, women are much better at showing vulnerability. I do think times are changing though – and I want to change too. It would be a lot better for everyone if men allowed themselves to burst into tears rather than burst into rage. Being a man can be a very lonely and destructive place, but it doesn't have to be.

*　　*　　*

Although I'm still fucking fuming on a daily basis for some reason or another, my anger has dissipated in the last few years. Part
of that is down to growing up, I think. As I've gotten older, I've
started to understand myself better. I've reflected on my life and
why I am the way I am. I've accepted that I feel every emotion,
even the ones I don't want to feel, at different levels, and they
have accumulated to become one cocktail of emotion. We all
have our own unique cocktails that lead us to our actions. I
never understood my specific blend before, but I've spent a lot
of time thinking about it and I think I have made more sense of
it now.

If you feel angry all the time, I think a good place to start is
getting in touch with your feelings. I know what you're thinking
– 'Don't be a wishy-washy fucker, Pete.' But seriously, we feel so
much shit every single day, but how often do we stop and actually think, 'What's bothering me? Why am I feeling the way I
am?' When I was writing this chapter, my friend told me about
something called the 'feelings wheel' that is often used in psychotherapy. You can look it up online, but it's basically this big
wheel with all different emotions, so you can really pinpoint
what you're feeling and why. So instead of just 'anger', maybe
you're feeling let down, humiliated, jealous, betrayed or bitter.
Once you can name that feeling, it could help you have a more
constructive conversation about whatever you're dealing with,
rather than just flying off the handle.

Most of us will have patterns in the things that make us angry.
For me, I hate feeling out of control and I hate feeling useless.
I know where that stems from – not feeling like I could help my

parents and not feeling like I was enough. And those feelings can reappear in the smallest ways, like when I misplace something, or a plan changes, or I see someone being a dickhead. It helps to remember that it's rarely about the specific thing and more about what's bubbling away under the surface.

Usually, my feelings of anger come back to self-loathing. And I think this is the same with a lot of people. I'm not really angry at the situation or even another person – I'm angry at myself. I hold myself to unrealistic standards of what I think I should be. I don't really blame other people for their shortcomings, but I think my own are the complete fucking end of the world. We'll go into self-worth more in the next chapter, but I'm telling you now because I think it's necessary to get a handle on why you might behave the way you do. For some people, that's going to therapy. For others, that's just spending some time with your own thoughts. For me, it has been a few years of mulling things over – and also writing this book. Maybe for you, it's talking to someone you trust. We could all do with investing some time into understanding ourselves better.

I think my anger also dissolved a bit when my nan died. Instinctively, that just made me much more in touch with the sadness that comes into my anger. I cry much more now. Something as simple as seeing an elderly lady on her own on a bus makes me want to cry. I know, I've become a wet flannel. But I think it has replaced those outbursts of anger, and I'm not ashamed of that. Instinctively, crying makes me feel ashamed and disappointed in myself. But I keep reminding myself that it's normal and okay to feel sad.

It's also that I just don't put myself in situations where I know I could combust. I only really socialise with the same people I trust, in venues where I know the people who run them and I feel safe. I try to control my environment, to a certain extent. That's why I'm known as 'Party Pete' among my friends, because I like to sort everything and have it all planned out. On the one hand, I think this is a positive step – you should take yourself away from situations that will make you angry. On the other hand, it pisses me off that I still don't trust how I could react to something. That, in itself, makes me feel pathetic. I want to be able to trust myself more, and that's something I'm working on.

Most of the time, when I feel angry now, I'll just swear a bit and let it out, but I try not to let it overwhelm me like it once used to. If I'm worried that the anger is starting to bubble up, I'm better at noticing it now, so I'll make an effort to do something that makes me feel happy and calm. I'll go on a walk with the dogs to clear my head or get outside on my motorbike. You have to recognise your own patterns before you know how to break them. This will look different for you. Maybe counting to ten will work for you or maybe speaking to someone will. For me, I like to be on my own. It's okay for you to have your own method of dealing with things, but work out your triggers and figure out what helps, and then you have an action plan ready to go.

Don't be disheartened if the first thing you try doesn't solve your problems. It can make you feel really fucking down when you try some kind of technique that worked for someone else and it doesn't for you, and then you think you're the problem and so you just give up. But it is always possible to find something that snaps you out of it. Don't accept defeat and think, 'I am what I am.' Yes, you'll probably always have certain triggers or knee-jerk reactions to things, but how you behave and how you grow can be within your control. You just have to keep trying.

Maybe you're reading this and thinking, 'I don't need advice about dealing with anger, but I do love someone who has a bad temper.' First of all, I'd say that no matter what shit they're dealing with, it is never, never okay for someone you love to take their anger out on you. Yes, I could be a little shit and got into fights here and there, but I can hand-on-heart say that I would only get into fisticuffs with someone who was an actual dickhead. I know that's still not an excuse because aggression is never the answer, but I just want to make it clear that if someone you love is hurting you (whether emotionally or physically), it ain't your fucking fault or responsibility to fix it. If you love someone, you would never want to hurt them, whether you're the angriest fucker in the world or not. The only thing you can really do in that situation is step away from them, and seek extra help if you feel like you need it.

But if you do love someone who just seems to be full of rage, if they raise their voice at the slightest inconvenience or perhaps take their anger out on walls, I have some suggestions for you. Firstly, accept that you'll never truly understand their inner workings. No matter how hard you try to understand someone, you'll probably fail. I know that sounds negative, but I think it will help you relinquish some kind of control or responsibility for the situation. It doesn't matter how long you've known someone, their moods will probably never make sense to you. But what you can do is just be there for them. I think that's probably what I've needed my whole life – for someone to just be there. Not to scold me for my behaviour or try to understand what I'm doing, but to just say: 'I know you're angry. I see you, and I'm here.' I know from living with my mum that she took a lot of the blame for how I behaved, but it wasn't one person's fault. I know some things had fucked me up to make me how I was, but it was also on me to tackle my demons myself. Whoever the individual is in your life, it's on them to make those changes.

Anger can be scary. Anger can be confronting. It's not easy to address this sort of shit, but I'm here doing it, and we all fucking should. It's fine to feel pissed off when the world doesn't go your way or when your mate sends you a five-fucking-minute-long voice note rambling on about absolute shite when you're too busy to listen. It's okay to get annoyed when your family members make backhanded remarks about your weight or why you're not married yet. This world is infuriating, and that's out of our control, but you deserve to find inner peace and not let all of these silly things control you.

Listen to what that anger is trying to tell you. Maybe the long voice note feels like such an affront because you just feel so busy and overwhelmed, and it's like one more fucking thing. Maybe those comments about your weight and eternal single status knock your self-esteem and make you feel shit about your life choices. Get to the root of those issues. Find a way through them. Anger in small doses isn't all bad – it can be useful if you harness it correctly.

Final Fucking Thoughts: Listen to what your anger is telling you

★ Get to know yourself in order to understand your anger triggers and why you feel the way you do. Expressions of anger often come from emotional repression.

★ Aggression ain't a sign of strength. We need to stop allowing toxic masculinity to hold us back.

★ I don't blame you for feeling angry at the world. The world is full of dickheads, but it's up to us how we respond.

CHAPTER 3

You're Worth More Than the Money You Make

Believe it or not, I had a proper career before I started making a prick of myself on telly. I've always been a grafter and have never needed to rely on anyone, which I take a lot of pride in. In fact, I started working when I was twelve years old, doing a couple of paper rounds. It was after my parents had split up and I knew my mum didn't have a lot of money, so I wanted to help her out. I was giving her money every week – it can't have been much, but it was something. Then, when I was thirteen, I started working at a local hotel. I just walked in there and asked if they had any work going; that was the kind of kid I was. I didn't enjoy school – the academic shit wasn't for me – but I knew I could put the work in, and I just wanted to earn money. As I mentioned before, I always thought I was older than I was, so working came more naturally to me as a kid than school did.

The hotel took me on as a glass collector, and then I ended up being a waiter at weddings and corporate events. By the age of sixteen, I was doing thirty to forty hours of work a week, on top of school. So I'd be working in the evenings, and then I'd do full shifts on Saturday and Sunday. The Sunday shifts were known as 'the graveyard shift' because it was always fucking dead, so I'd just sit around and then occasionally take some money from the till and use it in the fruit machines. If I lost, I'd just replace what I took with my own money. But if I won (and I was always chasing the win), then I'd have an extra forty quid on top of my six-pound-an-hour salary – happy days. I was always looking to make a bit of extra cash.

Working this young meant I grew up even quicker than I already was. I ended up being friends with everyone who worked at the hotel – they were all in their twenties and sometimes thirties. So I was going to pubs and clubs from the age of fifteen. I loved spending my own money and not having to ask anyone for whatever I needed. I know I wasn't earning much, but, at that age, it was alright. If I wanted a new pair of trainers, I could buy them myself. The other kids at my school were still getting pocket money and asking their parents for things. Not me – and that felt good. I was obsessed with being independent and I'm sure that mindset came from when I shut up shop after my dad left. I didn't want to need anyone emotionally – or financially. I never wanted to be a burden to anyone. I also just wanted to keep myself busy, to distract myself from all the shit going on in my head. I liked being out of the house. I'm still like that now, really; I use non-stop work and busyness as a coping mechanism.

But anyway, I fucking loved working at that hotel – I have some of the best memories from that time. My boss, John, was a fucking great guy. Sometimes, after weddings, we'd play golf across the stairs and have a drink together. And our team had this tradition that, when we were clearing up after a big event, if we found any money on the floor, we'd use it to buy lottery tickets. So one day, I got a text from John while I was at school, saying, 'Pete, we've won the lottery. Come down to the hotel tonight.' I can't tell you how excited I was to get that message. I thought, 'No fucking way.' I was going round telling everyone in school that I'd won the lottery. I genuinely thought I was going to be fucking off out of Essex and living on a luxury yacht in the Caribbean. So I got to the hotel and everyone's there, drinking and cheers-ing to our new-found wealth. But then I found out it was only £18,000, and split between everyone it was £2,000 each. I mean, £2,000 when you're a teenager is still a fucking lot of money, but I thought we had won millions.

Still, I put that money towards buying my own car – a Renault Clio Extreme. It said 'Extreme' on it, which was very important (it wasn't 'extreme' in any sense of the word, but I thought it was cool). I had passed my test before anyone else my age, and I loved driving around doing whatever the fuck I wanted to do, picking up my dates and then dropping them home again. I was always dating people who were older than me, somehow getting away with taking out girls in their twenties when I was only seventeen. I looked about thirty from when I was twelve, which was a blessing – but now I'm in my thirties, I look like I'm in my fifties. So it's swings and fucking roundabouts.

There was a lot of chat in my school about where people were going for sixth form, what they were going to study for A Levels and then which uni they'd go to. But I knew that path was never really for me. I was decent at Maths and English, but I hated sitting in the classroom and bunked off school all the time. I hate being told what to do, and I hate being forced into doing things. So I thought: 'Right, I'm going to get a stable, well-paid job where I can earn some fucking good money.' So, without much knowledge of what jobs were even out there, and knowing I was good with numbers, I settled on the idea of being an accountant. I printed off about thirty CVs that were obviously full of fucking shit – talking about all the times I helped with the books at the hotel (obviously not mentioning my use of the fruit machines) – and I drove around all the accountancy firms within half an hour of where I lived to hand them in. And because I've got the gift of the gab, I managed to swing myself a job at one of the firms. I didn't really need any qualifications at that point, since I started off as a tea boy. It was an apprenticeship type thing, and you were supposed to take the accountancy qualification – the AAT – at the end of it, but I still had it in my head that I could blag it without any qualifications. I was earning my first salary: £12,500 a year. It was hardly anything, but I was still a teenager and it felt like freedom.

I worked for that firm for almost two years and, I've got to be honest, it was really fucking boring. But I did learn a lot there. I worked for a great guy and all the people were really lovely. I learned how you have to adapt to an office environment and always make yourself useful and seem really enthusiastic. I was doing the donkey work, going through receipts and expenses for people, semi-learning the ropes. But I found out quickly that, although I was good with numbers and it was a stable career, I fucking hated the work. My favourite part of the day was my lunch break, and I'd be counting down the minutes until it arrived.

But every step – even the shittier ones – can get you closer to something better. While I was at that firm, I did some work for a recruitment company that specialised in healthcare, doing the accounts for them. I really got on with them, and they offered me a job to come and work for them. I had started learning more about what recruitment entailed and I liked the fact it was commission-based – so, the more people you can get hired, the more money you make. It's a good set-up if you know you're able to work hard, as you'll get rewarded for it. So I moved there, and realised recruitment was a pretty good gig for me. I've always been quite good at speaking to people and getting them on side, and the money from my commission started pouring in. The more I worked, the more I earned – and given I actually enjoyed working non-stop, this was fucking perfect for me.

That company was based in Hertfordshire – about a forty-minute drive from where I lived with my mum in Essex – but after about a year, I got head-hunted to work for a medical recruitment firm in the City, in London. I must have been about nineteen or twenty, moving into London for the first time, working in a job that allowed me to make some serious cash. My role was recruiting specialist consultant doctors to work in hospitals, and there weren't very many companies doing that at the time, which meant I was able to really get to know all the hospitals and all the doctors, and there was plenty of work to go around. The doctors were on high salaries too, which meant that my cut was fucking great. There was so much more opportunity to make money, and I fucking ran with it.

I was already good at building relationships, but I wanted to take that even further. I read books on neuro-linguistic programming (NLP), which is all about the power of persuasion. It's sort of Derren Brown shit, where you drop little cues into a conversation to make someone think they have come up with an idea by themselves. I know it sounds horrible, but I learned how to adapt myself to different situations and different people. I was working with a lot of well-educated, older people, so I taught myself to speak with a posher accent and make my voice lower too (which, apparently, makes people respect you more).

Although my clients might have believed I was an upstanding family man, I was actually living the ultimate city-boy lifestyle. I mean, what do you expect when a man who is barely in his twenties is earning a shit-ton of money? I worked hard, but I played even harder. At the time, my company was almost all-male, and there was a real culture of competition and going out non-stop. You'd finish work after a fifteen-hour day, then go to a bar, then a club, then a strip club (because they were always open until 6am), then you'd buy a new shirt on the way into work before arriving in the office at 8am, having a shower there and getting back to the grind. And then you'd go out and do it all over again. God knows how I had the stamina to keep going like that, but I think I was running off adrenaline. I could be a mess sometimes – there was the odd occasion I fell asleep in my suit in doorways or in train stations. But somehow, my work was never affected. I just kept earning more money and building more trust with my clients, and eventually I was growing my own team. I was barely twenty-one, but I was doing really fucking well for myself.

And with big money came big spending. I was a horrendous spender, buying cars, clothes and watches. The biggest waste of money was how much I spent on nights out – I basically threw thousands down the drain on tables, drinks and dinners. It was fucking ridiculous. The one thing I didn't really spend my money on was holidays, which, in hindsight, should've been the main thing I used it for. I think money is well-spent when you use it on experiences, but I was such a fucking workhorse that I would never let myself go away and actually rest. Instead, my money was just going on nights out that I'd barely remember the next day. I'm not sure I'd recommend it. I'm still like that today – I go to amazing places with the job I do now, but I rarely have a holiday.

That said, the money did have its perks. I had enough money to comfortably buy my nan a place when she came back from Spain, after she'd made a bad investment on a house out there and lost everything. It made me feel good that I was able to help her. That's got to be the main benefit of earning well: being able to help out the people you love. But I won't lie and say that it was completely selfless. I think I felt validated by the fact I was able to provide for my family. There's so much pressure for men to be providers, isn't there? I definitely grew up with the idea that men should earn well and look after the women in their lives – whether that's a wife or, in my case, my mum and my nan. I wanted to be the man of the house; someone they could rely on. My dad had done well for himself and my mum had given up work when she married him, so that was the blueprint I was working from. And, when he left, she really struggled to get back on her feet.

I had this idea that the men are supposed to go out and work, and the women stay home and look after the kids. That wasn't the kind of life I wanted, and I didn't expect that from a partner – I think ambition is one of the sexiest qualities in a woman – but it was something that had made its way into my head. I still always pay for everything when I take women on dates, even if they're much more successful than me. It's not about wanting to have the upper hand; it's just about feeling like I can provide something. Maybe having money, and spending it on other people, is a way to make myself feel useful. Again, I hate being a burden. And that all comes back to the deep sense of emptiness I have. Because if I can't offer drinks and lavish gifts and help with paying the mortgage, then what can I offer? Why would anyone want me around?

I think, when I was a kid, I thought that if I could just earn enough money and be 'successful', I'd be happy. I thought it was the secret to self-worth. But the reality is that the more you have, the more you want. There's a reason why rich people just get richer – it's because we live in a world of more, more, more. You can have everything you could ever possibly need, but there will always be something else you'll want. There's always a bigger yacht, or a bigger jet, or another watch you could buy. It never really ends.

We think that success equals money and money equals happiness. But the problem is, you reach the top of that mountain, where you achieve a goal or start earning six figures, and then you realise there's another, bigger mountain you want to climb. It's a real head-fuck because you think buying more stuff will make you happier, but it actually makes you unhappier. Because buying things is like a hit of dopamine – it makes you happy for a fleeting moment, but it doesn't last. And the more expensive the things you own, the less you appreciate them. I was so fucking excited to buy that first Renault, but when I was buying a Porsche, it didn't feel like such an accomplishment. I was just like, 'Oh yeah, this is what I'm meant to have.' It lost its shine. You end up buying things out of habit, chasing that hit of joy, rather than actually appreciating everything. It's fucked.

It all comes back to the title of this book – there is never enough material stuff to make you happy. You will always want something else. You'll always strive to earn more and spend more. Unless, that is, you break the cycle. I'm not sure when I realised that earning (and spending) money wasn't the be-all and end-all of life. I think it dawned on me slowly. I noticed that I was using my cash to chase happiness that just wasn't arriving. I'd spend a fucking fortune on nights out and try to make everyone happy, but I wasn't even enjoying it myself. I became a caricature of myself – I was 'Party Pete', always the one buying the fuck-off bottle of tequila, wearing the flashiest shoes and watch. And I thought – is this really who I am? Just some geezer who will buy champagne for the table and keep the party going? We'll talk more about how I used alcohol and partying as coping mechanisms later on, but money and my idea of 'success' was a coping mechanism too. My life of excess was an attempt to find happiness way before the days of TV, but I was looking for it in all the wrong places.

I could be the life and soul when I was buying nice things and going to expensive places, but I noticed that I was feeling really low and lonely when I was on my own. When I stripped back all the big spending and I had to be in my own head, I felt hollow. Trust me, there's no greater prison than your own mind. I began to understand that you can fill your soul with belongings, but it's still an empty existence. You can have the fullest wardrobe in the world, but that doesn't mean your heart is full. If anything, you're just full of shit – literally.

I've realised now that chasing success – in the earning sense – is just another way of looking for validation. I don't want to get all psychotherapy about this, but I think, subconsciously, I still really wanted to impress my parents, especially my dad. It's like when you break up with a partner, and you want to go to the gym and look good to show them what they're missing. I think it's the same thing when you become estranged from a parent. It was a motivating force for me, deep down – like, 'Look at me now Dad. Look how well I've done without you.'

It's also that I knew I would never be enough for him, so I was trying to be enough for myself. I was trying to build armour around me from all the money I earned – I thought it would make me invincible, like nothing could ever hurt me again. But the armour is shit. It doesn't work. If you don't invest in your own mental health, nothing on the outside matters. It's like if you build a house with the nicest wallpaper and furniture, but if the foundations are shit, it's just going to fall down. It doesn't matter how much investment you put into the decor, that house will crumble to the ground.

Now, I'm not saying that it isn't good to have goals and to want nice things. I think it's important to have aims and ambitions, and, fuck me, I love going shopping and buying stuff I want. If you want to buy that nice bag, and you've earned the money, then, by all means, go for it. But you have to understand that it's not the pinnacle of happiness, it is just another material thing. You have to understand that buying 'stuff' isn't going to fill whatever hole you have in your heart. I'm so fucking grateful for everything I have – I am so fortunate to live the life I do, and to be able to buy the things I want. And especially from working, now, in a job that is pretty fucking easy and a lot of fun. It's a nice life, and I would never complain about that. But the difference is I know that money isn't a replacement for a happy, fulfilled life. I have seen first-hand that some of the richest people I've met are some of the most miserable and empty. On the other hand, I've seen people who barely have a pot to piss in who are some of the happiest fuckers about. I think it's because they just embrace what they have – they aren't constantly looking for something bigger and better.

In the end, success is completely subjective. When you hear the word 'success', what do you picture? I think most of us imagine some arsehole wearing designer clothes, taking private jets everywhere. They wouldn't picture, for example, a single mum, who has raised three amazing kids to be happy and self-sufficient. Your mind doesn't go – 'That's a success.' But, fuck me, of course it is. It's a huge fucking success. How amazing that a person is able to do that, with all the odds stacked against them. What a fucking achievement. I think a lot of people have an inferiority complex over not being 'successful' because they're not out there living like they're on *Selling Sunset*, but that doesn't make those people more successful than you. Maybe it makes them richer, but not more successful. The word 'success' is actually defined as the accomplishment of an aim or purpose. When you look at that and think about your life, you have the power to define what success means to you. There are so many different ways of measuring it. Success isn't defined by the amount of zeros on your fucking bank balance.

Whether you are on track to be a CEO or you're struggling to make ends meet, we can all take the time to be grateful for what we have along the way. You can hope for more, while still being happy with what you have now. I know some people write things like gratitude lists – where you write something you're grateful for every day, whether that's as grand as a new sofa or as small as your partner making you a cuppa in the morning. It can make you feel positive about all the things you do actually have, instead of thinking about all the shit you don't or want to have. I won't lie, writing a gratitude list isn't the kind of thing I'd do, but I do try to think of something I'm grateful for every day, just to train my brain in that direction, and it can be really simple, like being with my dogs. It will be different for everyone.

We need to start building up our self-worth from the inside, rather than leaning on external things to make us feel like we're

Me on
fireworks
night

Me in a hat

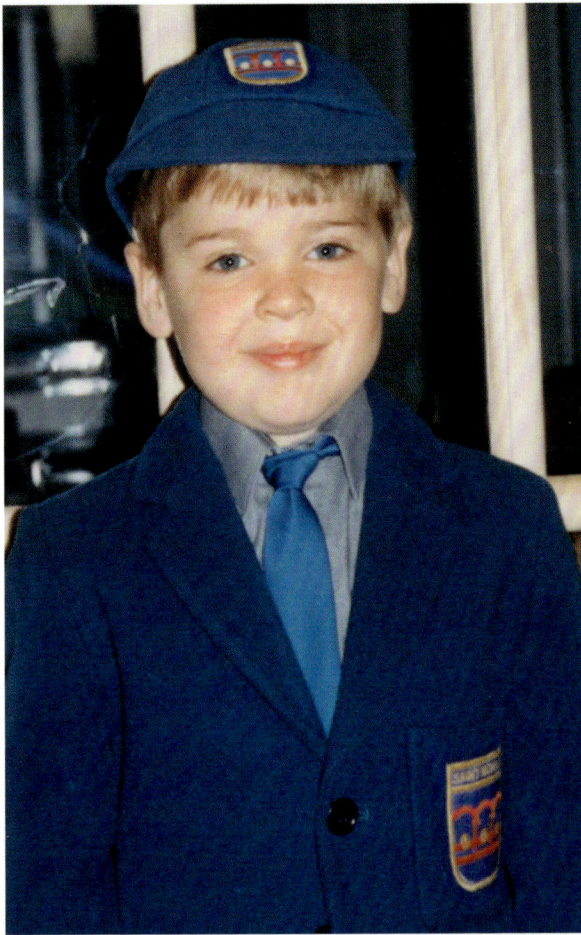

First day
of school

Me at my dance exam (I'm number 31)

Receiving a sports award

My first rescue dog, Arnie

Best pals

Me on holiday

Mum turns forty

So much love

With the *TOWIE* boys (Dan, Lockie and Diags) in our heyday

Me being fucking great at canoeing on *TOWIE*

Happiest on a bike

Got bitten by a baby shark on *Celebrity Island* with *Bear Grylls*

Celebrity Island tested my limits, but I loved it

Made a friend for life in the legend that is James Cracknell

worth something, especially at a time where we are all bombarded online about what a perfect life looks like. But how do you do that? I think it's about congratulating yourself and giving yourself credit for all the things you are good at and all the things you've achieved – even if, for you, that's just getting through the day. If you struggle with depression or you've been unwell, waking up for a shower can be the hardest fucking thing to do. But everything's relative; even the smallest acts can be achievements.

Look, I know first-hand that it's hard to be nice about yourself. I find it so fucking easy to see the best in my friends – I can compliment other people no end, but I struggle to do that for myself. I think it's because we all know too much about ourselves. We have been there through every single mistake, every single fucking failure, that we overlook the good things. They get overruled by the negative shit. It's so much easier to see the positive in the people you love because their good qualities radiate out to you. But it's fucking hard to see it in yourself. I'm not saying you should love yourself more than anyone and think you're God's gift to humanity – that's a one-way ticket to becoming an arrogant bastard. I just think we have to believe we're worthy of the same love we give to other people. But wow, that's something I really struggle with. I think everyone is worthy of love . . . except me. So maybe I'm telling this to myself as well, as a reminder. I need to take my own fucking advice.

I might seem like a hypocrite because I come across as so confident, when really my self-worth is on the fucking floor. Once I realised that money and a well-paid job wasn't the answer to self-worth, I didn't know what I was left with. So now I'm trying to build that from the ground up. While writing this chapter, my editor asked me to name one good thing about myself. I'd just been blabbing on about how you have to give yourself credit for all the good shit you do, but when she asked me that question, I thought: fuck. It was a complete mental block. I couldn't think of a good thing if my life depended on it.

How fucked up is that? To not be able to name a single thing you like about yourself? It was a bit of a reality check, to be honest. Because that's not how I want to be. It's not about being cocky, it's just about showing yourself some respect. So now, every week, I try to think of one good thing about myself. Like the other day, I helped some kid who ran into my garden because he was being chased. That was nice of me. Fuck, writing this book is a good deed. I'm trying to help people here – I'm trying to do something valuable. Who knows if it will be, but here I am, giving myself some credit.

Sometimes you have to get out of your own head and pretend you're speaking to yourself like you'd speak to a friend. Trust me, it works. So go on – think about one good fucking thing about yourself. If you can't think of anything, take that as a sign you need to get to know yourself better. Because I can promise you there are hundreds of great things about you that make you unique. Maybe you don't think there are, but there are. We take all sorts of skills for granted, like, for example, maybe you're really good at reading how other people are feeling. Or you're always the one who remembers to buy more toothpaste and toilet roll at home. They might seem basic to you, but lots of people are actually really shit at a lot of these things. Even the tiniest things are worth something – you just have to believe that. If you're really struggling to think of anything, ask those closest to you about what they think. But instead of being humble and resisting it, take the fucking compliment. Absorb what other people think about you, and actually make a conscious effort to believe it.

You might be thinking: why bother with this shit? Why do I need to build my sense of self-worth? It's because when something in life goes wrong, your self-worth is the first thing to go down the drain. If you lose your job or your relationship ends, you probably have a tendency to think there's something intrinsically wrong with you. It's easy to be a happy chappy when everything's going well, but self-worth can depreciate in the blink of an eye. So you have to keep building it up to give yourself that safety net if something goes badly. Part of self-worth is being able to say: 'I've made mistakes. That thing didn't work out. But I am still good enough. I am still worth something.' It's not pinning your entire sense of self on a certain career, a particular person or a specific amount of money in your bank account. Because that shit doesn't last forever. The only relationship you're guaranteed to have until the day you die is the one you have with yourself. You have to pick yourself up and remember who you are, and all the things that make you special. It's about finding the 'but'. 'My relationship ended but . . . I still have so many amazing friends.' 'I lost a load of money but . . . I still have great potential to earn more and get back on my feet.' Life is all about finding big buts (and I cannot lie).

Ultimately, a lot of this shit comes back to living in the moment and appreciating what you have now. You're not going to reach some kind of paradise once you get that pay rise or buy that pair of expensive shoes. I know it's a fucking cliché, but you have to enjoy the journey too. You don't want to waste your life obsessing over things. In the end, you'll leave this planet and all the shit you bought will be gone. At your funeral, no one's going to say, 'He owned a Rolex.' They're going to talk about the kind of person you were, whether you were kind to people and the stuff you put your energy into. Money should allow you to feel comfortable and help you solve problems, like buying your way out of a fucking parking ticket, but any more than that is meaningless. I'm saying this through gritted teeth: 'I'm worth more than all of that shit. I'm enough as I am.' If I can say that, you fucking can too.

Final Fucking Thoughts: You're worth more than the money you make

★ We know too much about ourselves, which means it's too easy to be self-critical. The trick is to talk to yourself like you'd talk to your mates.

★ Having self-worth ain't about thinking you're God's gift to the world. It's just about treating yourself with a little fucking respect.

★ Happiness doesn't come from having more stuff – it comes from appreciating what you already have.

CHAPTER 4

No One Is Better Than You, and You're Better Than No One

L et's address the elephant in the room: you're probably only reading this book because you know who I am, or someone who knows who I am bought this book for you. You probably wouldn't give a fuck about what I have to say otherwise, which is fair enough. (You probably shouldn't anyway, but thanks for being here regardless.)

I don't like to call myself 'famous' or a 'celebrity'. First of all, it makes me sound like a knob-head and, secondly, I haven't really done anything that warrants fame – I'm not a talented singer, actor or athlete. In fact, I'm not good at many things, except chatting bollocks all day. I have somehow become 'known' (yeah, let's use the word 'known') for just being myself. And I think this actually makes me pretty qualified to talk about the topic for this chapter: authenticity. I am a living, breathing, OG of reality TV and I am here to tell the tale and give my pennies' worth.

When you think about reality TV, 'authentic' might be the last word that comes to mind. I don't blame you. Because the genre is now so huge, it's sort of become the opposite of what it was intended to be – real people just living their real lives – because so many people apply to these shows hoping for fame and fortune, and are often anything but authentic. They want the Instagram followers and the fashion partnerships and for their five fucking minutes in the sidebar of shame. But back when I started on *TOWIE* in 2015 – when it was on its fifteenth season – it wasn't like that (at least, not as much). There weren't many people making a lot of money from reality TV at that time; most people just did it for a laugh, taking it day by day with no blueprint for having some big career off the back of it.

That's what happened for me, anyway. I fell into *TOWIE* sort of by accident. I had been working in the City for years by that point, and had been burning the candle at both ends for far too long. I was taking some time out and, thankfully, I'd done well enough for myself to be able to afford to do that. My plan was eventually to get back to the grind, maybe at a different company or starting my own business, but I was taking a break first. And it was at this point that my friend Lockie, who had been on *TOWIE* for a few seasons by then, asked if I wanted to join for an episode. I thought, 'Why the fuck not? I've got nothing better to do.'

My first scene in *TOWIE* was at a pool party in Marbella. I had to walk through the party and everyone was like, 'Who the fuck is that?' because most of the cast didn't know me. I also looked a bit different to your typical person from Essex at that time, with my man-bun and head-to-toe tattoos. In my first scene, I was just having a chat with Lockie with our legs dangling into the pool. I wasn't nervous in front of the cameras – I was accustomed to performing, in a way, for all my clients in my City job. I also hadn't ever watched *TOWIE*. In fact, I hadn't watched any reality TV and I still haven't. I think this is important as it means I have never become a self-dialoguing actor – essentially someone who acts a certain way to create a role or persona for themselves. It's probably why I've been loved and hated at different times – because I'm always just being myself. And that's actual reality: most of us are good and bad at different points. Most people don't fit into solid 'villain' and 'hero' categories (some do, mind you, but I ain't naming names). Anyway, I also just thought it would be a laugh. I wasn't taking it too seriously or worrying about how I was coming across.

After that scene, the producers were like, 'You're not bad at this,' and so I carried on filming for the rest of the Marbella episodes. At the time, *TOWIE* was filmed about a week or two before it aired on TV. While we were filming, I was papped hanging out with the cast. So, before my first episode even aired, I was all over the press, with people being like, 'Who's this new guy?' I was booked to do my first PA (public appearance) before I was even on TV. These were basically club appearances – it was how reality TV people made money before social media came into play. You'd get paid to go to a party and say hello to people. It was wild how quickly people wanted to come out to see me. I couldn't believe it.

Given my presence on the series had caused a stir before the first episode even aired, the production team invited me to stay on as a regular cast member. I knew I had enough contacts and cash behind me that, if reality TV didn't work out for me, I'd be absolutely fine. I could start a company and go back to my normal life. There was no pressure and no expectation. I just thought I'd give it a go and potentially have a fun summer.

Looking back, I know I was lucky to be joining a structured reality show like that in its golden age. At the time, there was only really us, *Made in Chelsea* and *Geordie Shore*. Now, there are so many shows, it's like a revolving door of reality stars, and it's harder to break through. Not that I was really trying to break through; I was just enjoying it for what it was.

We got to do some amazing things, like flying out to Thailand – it was basically just a big holiday with my mates, except we were being filmed and paid for it. The money wasn't much, mind – you'd mostly make money off things you did on the side. For me, it was a fuck-ton of PAs. I became known as 'PA Pete' as I genuinely really enjoyed doing them. I said yes to almost everything, so I was travelling up and down the country showing up at clubs all over the UK, sometimes three or four times a week. Often I'd be out partying all night, and then show up for filming straight away the next day. I mean, it wasn't that different from my City lifestyle really. I'd already experienced life in the fast lane and going to nice places, so suddenly becoming a TV person didn't actually feel that different. The main difference was just that I was working much less hard in between all the partying and more people knew who I was. I would show up to my PAs and people would be queueing around the block. Sometimes there were people crying or even fainting. I was so humbled that people wanted to queue to see me. I would think, 'Why the fuck do you care about me?' It was proper wild shit.

People still ask me about what *TOWIE* was really like and whether it was actually scripted. I know, some of that drama just seemed so extreme you'd think it was made up. But I promise you, every single relationship, argument and friendship was genuine. That said, although there was no script, storylines were important. The producers would need to know what was happening in everyone's lives and what they were talking about, and then they'd set up scenes for the conversations to take place. So you'd get a message telling you that you needed to show up at a certain time and place, and they'd tell you a dress code, whether that's night-time glam, casual, sportswear or whatever. They wouldn't say who you were meeting, but you could sometimes work it out by messaging your mates and asking if they'd received the same info. If none of the people I was friends with had got the message, I'd be like: 'Oh God, what's this about then?'

If you're not getting on with someone or there's some kind of drama, guaranteed you'd be meeting that person. So, in that sense, although the dialogue was all real, you'd be put in situations that wouldn't necessarily happen in ordinary life. Like, I wouldn't go out of my way to speak to someone who had been talking shit behind my back. But then I'd end up meeting them in the street, so of course it would kick off.

They'd do this thing called 'assumed knowledge', where everyone would have a right to reply if someone else had said something bad about you in earlier filming. They'd show you the clip. Then when you go into the scene, you could say, 'I heard you've been saying this.' It gives everyone the right to defend themselves and address it. But it's also, essentially, a way of creating storylines. There was a lot of he-said, she-said and, seeing how much people loved *TOWIE* at the time, clearly it made for great TV.

Every scene would end up being about three minutes long, but you'd normally film for about an hour. So they'd substantially cut down conversations. The producers want to make an interesting show, so obviously they're going to use the bit you don't like – it was sometimes frustrating. But you have to take responsibility for the shit you do when you're being filmed. You signed up to that, so that's on you. If you say something rude, that's your fucking fault.

I was a producer's dream and nightmare at the same time. I was a dream because I was always so fucking opinionated, but also a nightmare because, towards my last four or five years, I said I didn't want to be briefed. Though they'd never tell people directly what to say, they'd definitely stir the pot a bit. Before you'd go into each scene, they'd give you a quick brief, saying 'remember all this happened' . . . But I wanted to show up and just react to whatever was happening at the time. By that point, they'd just put me in a scene because they knew I'd have an opinion. I had already earned my stripes, as I seemed to be involved in everything in my first few years because I was always having a romance or fucking something up.

However, I never went out of my way to create a storyline. Along the way, people would try to create storylines from nothing because they had fuck-all else going on. The more you're involved in stuff, the more work you get. But with such a big cast and so many people fighting for airtime, if you're not fucking interesting, that's your fucking problem. I didn't have a lot of respect for people like that because it wasn't genuine. I seemed to find myself in a lot of shit naturally, which wasn't always a good thing, but that's just how it was.

I think I was different to a lot of reality people in that I probably got on better with the producers and crew than I did with the cast. Throughout my whole career in TV, they're the people I want to go for a drink with. I've been so fortunate to work with great people behind the scenes. I've always had the mentality that the crew are just as, if not more, important than the people you see on screen. It's a joke that the cast were always called 'the talent' when we didn't have a shred of talent between us. And yet some of the cast could be complete and utter divas.

Interestingly, I've noticed that the people on screen who don't seem as likeable are actually the more genuine, authentic, nice people. I've worked with people over the years who you'd think are wonderful, but they're actually total c*nts. I've seen people shout in runners' faces for getting coffee orders wrong, or clicking their fingers at people. It's like, who the fuck do you think you are? But, thankfully, the arseholes tend not to get as much work because everyone talks – that junior runner five years ago could be a big-shot producer now, and they won't work with you if you screamed at them for no reason. I know, in this industry, we work long hours and everyone has good and bad days, but that's never an excuse to be a dick. I have a dry sense of humour and I take the piss, but if I ever offended someone I worked with I'd be absolutely mortified and gutted. I think the reason I'm still kicking about in this industry is because I try to be nice to everyone, and have formed genuinely good relationships with people. And that's sound advice for every job you do. It shouldn't be fucking hard to be nice.

You also still need a solid work ethic to make it. I'm not going to say this job is the hardest in the world because I know it fucking isn't, but you do still need to perform. You live and die by your last job, so you can't really have an 'off' day. You have to be on, the best you can, non-stop. It's about having pride in what you do, no matter how silly, and always showing up to something that you say you're going to be at. I think I have always had that mentality, ever since I did that paper round: work ethic is something you've either got or you ain't. If I lost everything tomorrow and had to take whatever job I could get, I'd do it to the absolute best of my ability. It doesn't matter what you do, it's about doing it as best you can and not letting people down.

Anyway, back to *TOWIE*. I got a reputation for being a bit of a Lothario fairly early on. I was dating women on the show, and I think the first stories about me in the tabloids were from women I had slept with in my City days who had sold their stories – it would be about their 'night of passion with Pete Wicks' or something ridiculous like that. It didn't bother me. Back then, it wasn't the worst thing to be known as. And, to be honest, it was fucking true. I wasn't trying to be a villain or anything like that, but I had always enjoyed going on dates and, unsurprisingly, the press latched on to that.

While I was on *TOWIE*, I had probably one of my most

controversial relationships. By the way, this girl is still one of my really good friends and I think she's amazing.

At first, we had a great relationship, but the tide started to turn a few months in. We hadn't been dating long, but it was the first relationship I'd had in the public eye and it was intense. I'm not saying we were like Posh and Becks, but sometimes it felt a bit like that – there was a lot of scrutiny on us and everything we did, and there were people following us and trying to take pictures. I found that really hard to deal with because it wasn't just me, it was my relationship and I wasn't really able to separate TV Pete from the real Pete. Before this girlfriend, I felt like I did a good job at not making *TOWIE* my entire life. I never had any of my relatives on the show and I never let them film at my house. I wanted to keep parts of my private life hidden, so that at least when people criticised me, I could just say: 'Ah well, they're only seeing part of what I'm putting out. They don't know me.'

That wasn't really possible anymore when I was with her, as the lines became very blurred. Plus, she was probably even more opinionated than me, so, if she had a disagreement with someone, I'd back her. We fell out with a lot of people. If it wasn't her in a drama, it was me – so we were in double the amount of fucking drama. Shall I say 'drama' again? But it's wild because, behind closed doors, we were sweet and we had a great time together. We were like best friends.

I'm not going to try to justify all the shit that went down with me and my ex, but I will just say that there was more happening behind the scenes that people don't know about, and that I won't speak about either, because it's not fair. And I do take full responsibility for my colossal fuck-up – which was sending explicit messages to another girl. My ex actually already knew there had been messages, and it was something we were dealing with in private. But when someone sold stories on the messages I'd sent, suddenly our dirty laundry was being aired for everyone to see. It all came out when we were filming in Marbella. The producers caught wind of it first, so they changed the entire day of filming so that I could film a scene with my girlfriend responding to the scandal. We hadn't discussed the scene beforehand, so it was completely raw and real. I know it's what we signed up for, but, fuck me, it was brutal. Like: 'This is what's happened – your girlfriend has just found out your graphic messages have been leaked to the press. Have a chat about it with ten cameras pointed at you, GO!'

When that happened, I went from being loved to hated overnight. The press had an absolute fucking field day, and the level of abuse, hatred and trolling I received was mind-blowing. I had people shouting at me in the streets, someone spit in my car when I had the window rolled down. I had people telling me to die of cancer and that I should go and kill myself. I had people sending me videos of dolls they'd made to look like me, hanging them in the street and then burning them. Once, when I was on a dog walk, I had someone say that if they ever saw me again they would kick me and my dogs to death. It was a lot. I felt like the most hated person in the UK.

The impact was massive. I lost work because of it. I was

barely eating, and I was boozing excessively. I was basically just getting by. I consider myself a strong person, but I had never felt so low because I just couldn't see a way out. I thought that was gonna be it for the rest of my life, and I'd be forever known as the guy who fucked over his girlfriend. Realistically, there were millions of people out there who did not give a shit about me or my life, but when you're receiving thousands of messages and trolling on social media every day, it's all-consuming. And it was so hard to still be doing the show and giving people more ammo, when I couldn't do or say anything right. I apologised over and over, but it didn't seem to make anything better.

My nan helped me get through that time. She was the only person I could talk to who didn't judge me. She'd tell me I was a fucking dickhead because she was always honest, but that people make mistakes. Weirdly enough, I also had my relationship to lean on. Throughout the whole thing, we were still best friends. We would row all the time, but we were the only ones who understood what we were going through. It was all very toxic and wild, but I know it was also a horrendous time for her, and I tried to make her feel better too. I knew I had fucked up in a big way, but she was the only person I felt guilty about hurting. Realistically, it was no one else's fucking business. But, at the same time, I thought: 'I have to just take it.' I think a part of me welcomed the negativity because I thought I deserved the vile treatment I received. Not just for the messages, but for who I am as a person. It confirmed everything I already believed about myself.

All that did was close me off emotionally, even more than I already was. I became so much more guarded. I want to be really clear how blessed I am, and my life in the spotlight has generally been pretty sweet. People have a lot harder fucking lives and I would never make out otherwise. But when you receive that level of abuse and you're scrutinised for everything, including showing emotion, you just go into survival mode. I thought: people only want me when they can see the good sides, and not the bad or the ugly. I think that has filtered out into my personal life too because I don't like being around people when I'm not happy. But anyway, we'll get into that more later on.

I can't pinpoint a particular moment, but eventually all the madness died down. I think it was probably after a year. I guess people have short memories and just latch on to whatever the latest drama is. My ex did forgive me, but, after a while, the pressure of the public relationship was too much and it was never really going to work. We're still friends now though – we even both ended up on *Celebs Go Dating* a few years later, being wingmen for each other. Even though it felt like I had lost all dignity and respect in the public forum, she still saw the best in me and knew what I was really like. It's nice to know that, now all the shit is said and done. And I know I would never behave like that again. I have a lot of regrets from my life about the ways I've treated people, but don't we all? It's all about owning up to your mistakes and learning to live with them.

I've never had a particularly good rapport with the press – they've fucking hounded me since day one. It doesn't matter how much I have changed, I will still always be 'Love Rat Pete

Wicks'. When you're on TV, you become a caricature of yourself, and it's hard to escape these identities that are pinned on you. It means that, even now, there'll be a headline about me doing something with a dog charity and the headline will be like, 'Love Rat Pete Wicks Saves Dog'. I know I can't complain because I put myself in a position to be talked about, but it's still annoying. Especially with online articles, they all have these clickbait headlines and most people won't even read the actual story. People will make their mind up about you from the first few words.

Obviously the press is so important for things that are actually in the public's interest, and it's amazing for raising awareness about issues, but there's an element of entertainment to it that is quite sadistic. It acts as an escape for people to look at other people's lives while not having to look at their own. It's voyeurism, isn't it? It's like how everyone always slows down on the motorway to look at a car crash – that's what reading the gossip news is like, and social media has made that even more intense; just watching a car crash from a distance, from the comfort of your own fucking car, without any regard for the people actually involved in the crash. I don't blame the journalists who write this stuff. I know a lot of journalists and they're not bad people – they're only writing things that people want to read, which is their job. But you have to understand that it's not all fucking gospel. Any woman I am spotted with becomes a 'mystery woman', including people I work with, and my friends' fucking wives and girlfriends.

As someone who has been on the receiving end of a fuck-ton of bad publicity, the saying 'all publicity is good publicity' is utter rubbish. The only way I've been able to handle it is by remembering that the only opinions that matter are the ones that come from people I care about and who care about me. Public opinion can hurt, but I no longer let it dictate my life. No matter how much people think they know me, they never really will. But it's okay – we don't need to know everyone to their core, especially 'celebrities' or whoever else. We can just focus on the people we love in our real lives and on being who we are. Now, I let the clickbait headlines and negative Instagram comments wash over me because I know I am authentic with my family, my friends, the people I meet and with myself. I have the power not to be who they say I am. I have control over who I actually am – and you have the same. You are so much more than the perfect (or not-so-perfect) pictures. You are so much more than whatever they say you are.

It's also important to acknowledge that I've had some fucking great feedback, and I'm honoured that people like watching me or listening to me. I'm in a very fortunate position to be able to make people laugh or brighten up their days, and I don't take that for granted. I really don't. I'd be lying if I said it was selfless too – it's nice to be liked and validated. But at the same time, if you don't listen to all the negative shit, you also shouldn't listen to all the positive shit too much. It's just two extremes. People will love you and hate you, but you have to remember that you're somewhere in the middle.

Maybe I'm wrong, but, in my opinion, 'fame' hasn't affected

my ego. I think people have an idea of me as arrogant because I have an 'I don't give a fuck' air about me. This is far from reality, and I've always had family and friends around me who would make sure I never get too big for my boots. My nan always said: 'No one's better than you, and you're better than no one.' I will remember that my whole life because it's true: our social status or how many fucking Instagram followers we have doesn't matter. The sooner you recognise that you're no better, and no worse, than anyone else, the easier life becomes.

I know it's pretty unusual to have stuff written about you in the press or to be stopped in the street. But the issues of 'fame' are really just extreme versions of the shit we all have to deal with. We all have times when we feel misrepresented and misunderstood in our everyday lives, and when our reputations are tattered and our egos bruised. Most of us try to put out the best image of ourselves to other people. In the end, we all want to feel seen and known by other people, but, generally, that's just for our own social circles and family, rather than the whole of the UK. We all have times when we think: 'Who the fuck am I? Am I really what they think I am?' That's normal. It's just part of being a person.

That said, social media (aka the fucking devil) makes all this a million times worse. There's so much pressure now to show the best side of yourself; you think you have to look cool or hot or rich or whatever else. What this means is you basically end up living for other people instead of doing what you actually like and what makes you happy. You choose what to wear and where to go based on what people will think of you. How many people do you know who say they're going travelling to 'find themselves', but really it's just because they want to post all their lovely beach pictures and make other people jealous? Probably half the people you follow. How many times have you posted a selfie because you feel shit about yourself and you want the validation of watching the likes pour in? Probably more times than you'd want to admit.

Look, it's okay if you do that. I'm not blaming you if you love social media. I mean, I use it all the time too – I basically have to for work, but I do think I'd be happier if I could live off-grid. In the meantime, I think we all need to build healthier relationships with it. It causes so much comparison and makes us feel dissatisfied with our own lives and our own selves. I think one of the most authentic things you can do is live for the present, rather than doing it for everyone on social media to say it's amazing. It's sad that so many of us feel so reliant on other people's thoughts and opinions to feel good about ourselves.

So, with all that said, how can we be our most authentic selves? Number one: make peace with the fact you'll always be judged in some way. You can't please all of the people all of the time. Not everyone is going to like your life choices, but they also won't understand the backstory, or know the truth, or want the truth. If you surrender to the fact that not everyone will get you, it'll make your life a lot easier. People will like you and people will hate you, and some people just don't care, and that's okay.

I think there's an assumption that people who drastically change their style or the music they're into, or clean up their act, or whatever, are somehow becoming fake. But that's wild to me because we all change all the time – emotionally, socially, internally, externally; it doesn't make us any less authentic. And that change can be beautiful – like a butterfly starting off as a fucking caterpillar. Being open to changing your mind is probably one of the biggest signs of true authenticity. That, alongside vulnerability, transparency and integrity. It's just about meaning what you say, saying what you mean and not being so affected by other people's perceptions.

When it comes to style, I think the important thing is to go with what feels good in the moment. I've been told I have quite an authentic look, but I never set out to be the geezer with the long hair and tattoos – it just happened that way. I tried things and decided I liked them, and that's what stuck. People often question my fashion choices, but I just pick what I like and, if other people don't like what I'm wearing, they can fuck off. They don't have to wear it, and that's fine. I think authentic style is all about just choosing things you like, not because they're trendy at the time, and wearing whatever you've chosen with confidence.

The other misconception people have about authenticity is that it's all about being really 'different'. But I've met a lot of people who are quite . . . alternative, shall we say, but there's nothing authentic about them. Sometimes it's just a statement to say, 'Look at me, I'm going against the grain.'

Meanwhile, people who don't dress or do anything out of the ordinary are some of the most genuine people about because they're comfortable in who they are and they're not constantly trying to prove something. It's all about the thought process behind it.

True authenticity isn't about saying, 'I don't give a fuck about what anyone else thinks.' You can still have respect for other people and be adaptable around who you're with – it doesn't make you any less authentic. I can be a bit of a chameleon, but I don't think that's a bad thing. We all have different versions of ourselves, depending on who we're around. I am a slightly different person around my mum, compared to people I work with, compared to who I am when I'm dating. It's normal to care about what other people think. Understanding and taking on board everyone's point of view, and what's appropriate for a situation, doesn't make you any less authentic or genuine – it just means you have empathy, emotional intelligence and awareness. Don't let anyone tell you that you should just bulldoze your way through life without having any regard for the people around you. That doesn't make you unique or special – it just makes you rude.

We all have identities, or narratives, that we're lumped with for years and find it difficult to escape from. Maybe you were always drunk at parties when you were at school and your schoolmates still continually refer to you as 'the mess' fifteen years on. Or your parents still call you a fussy eater because you didn't like carrots aged five. We are all assigned roles and identities because we like categorising things and people. For some reason, our culture isn't so accepting of the idea that people grow and change. I don't want the same things as I did when I first went on *TOWIE*. I don't want to be a 'love rat' anymore. I'm in my thirties and would like to settle down and all that crap (whether I'm capable of it is a story for another chapter, but still). Maybe it's hard for me to break out of that title because I'm 'known', but this shit is hard for everyone.

'Be yourself' is the most clichéd saying, but, weirdly, it can be one of the hardest pieces of advice to follow. Being yourself should be the easiest thing in the world, but it actually doesn't come naturally to most people. That's because of so many things: pressure from other people, and the pressure we put on ourselves. We're social creatures and we'll always be affected by shit going on around us. I think, one day, my dream would be to live completely off-grid in a cabin in the woods with my dogs. But I also know it would be difficult leaving the world I'm in now. I appreciate every single thing 'fame' has given me – I'm incredibly lucky, and I'm even thankful for the hard times because I've learned so much about myself. At the end of the day, I know who I am. It's not always good – sometimes it's pretty fucked up, actually. However, I'm constantly trying to be better and I'm being honest with myself about what I want and what matters to me. I am more or less the same person on and off camera, even if I do keep some things private. So, am I some dickhead who does fuck-all on TV? Yes. Am I a notorious ladies' man? I guess a bit, although I'm trying not to be. Despite all that crap, I am who I am. I'm not the best bloke in the world, but I'm not the worst either.

Final Fucking Thoughts: No one is better than you, and you're better than no one

★ 'Be yourself' should never be an excuse to be a dickhead. You can stay true to yourself while also being adaptable and respecting people around you.

★ There ain't nothing wrong with changing yourself. It's more authentic to shift and grow than to always stay the same.

★ There will be people who love you and people who hate you, but neither of these opinions tell the whole story about who you are.

CHAPTER 5

Even Lone Wolves Need Company

W hen I was a kid, my mum used to say she could take me anywhere and I'd happily go off and find some mates in the playground. She also used to throw a lot of parties at home, and I was quite content making conversation with the adults while all the other kids were outside in the garden. Basically, I was like Stewie from *Family Guy* – that annoying fucking kid hanging about. I'd be like, 'Alright Dave, how have you been, how's the wife?' And they'd be like, 'You're six years old, what does it matter to you, you fucking weirdo?' I guess I've always been interested in people and found it easy to make friends with lots of different types of people; it doesn't matter their age, background or whatever, I'm always up for having a chat and getting to know someone's story.

And if I end up considering you a friend, I would do fucking anything for you. It's one thing I really pride myself on – being a good mate is important to me. Some of my friends call me 'Daddy Pete', which I promise isn't as sexual as it sounds. It's just because I like to look after everyone on a night out, and insist all the girls message me when they get home safe. I want my friends to be happy and have a good time, but I also want them to know I'm always there to lend an ear if they need it.

I'd say all of that shit comes naturally to me, but what I find harder is letting other people be good friends to me. I'm really lucky to be surrounded by some fucking amazing people (some of whom you'll know, some of whom you won't; I have friends from all walks of life). But I'm guilty of not always noticing that love and allowing it in.

I view myself as a bit of a lone wolf. Even though I come across as a really sociable, confident person, I'm also quite introverted. I'm an outgoing loner, shall we say. I really need alone time to recharge and I tend to keep certain things to myself. I mean, my best mate hasn't even come round to my house, which I know a lot of people find weird. I think it's because, since being in the public eye, I've had to give so much of myself away and I like to keep some things sacred for myself.

Turning inwards isn't necessarily a bad thing – it's okay to be introverted and need your own space. Some people aren't comfortable enough with their own company, which I think is a shame. But the problem is, if you retreat too much, you can get into a cycle of aloneness that can lead to loneliness if you're not careful. So I'm writing this chapter to remind you (and myself – again, fucking hypocrite over here) why friendship is important and that it's okay to let other people in.

I'm aware that friendship is quite a difficult topic for a lot of people. I know loads of people who grew up being bullied or having issues with friends leaving them out or making them feel bad. Thankfully, I never had any experiences like that. I think it's partly because I started working when I was really young, so I had a whole world and friendship group outside of school. I think friendship groups that are formed in school can often contain a real mismatch of characters because you're forced together, rather than actually finding each other, getting along and choosing to stick around. I'm not saying you can't make lifelong friends in school – I have some mates I'm still in touch with, and I know other people who are still tight as fuck with their schoolmates. But the people you meet when you're young aren't the be-all and end-all. You'll come across lots of people throughout your life who might be better suited to you than the kids you were forced to sit next to in Science class. We're fed quite unrealistic stories about friendship: that once we're friends with someone, that's it – best friends forever. Sometimes it works like that, sometimes it doesn't. And if it doesn't, you're not a failure and there ain't something wrong with you. Some people come into your life for a moment in time, while others come into your life and stick around like a bad smell forever. But anyway, I'm going off topic.

As I said before, working in that hotel as a teenager meant I made friends who were a lot older than me. I've always felt really comfortable around people who had more years on me. I think it's because they have more life experience and wisdom. I believe you should learn things from your friends; they should offer a unique perspective and challenge you a bit. I always find it so sad and boring when I see friendship groups out in the wild and they all look, dress and sound exactly the same. You don't just want to surround yourself with 'yes' men who blow smoke up your arse (although I sadly know a lot of people in my industry who do that).

When I was young, I wasn't interested in gossip and fallouts, the 'he said this' and 'she said that', and all that toxic shite. I learned a lot from my older pals about what friendship is. I was the baby of the group and I couldn't drive for a while, and they'd be like, 'Pete, don't worry about it, I'll drop you home.' I think that's an important part of a friendship – that you can compensate for each other's weaknesses and help each other out, without ever expecting anything in return. They made an effort to involve me and look out for me, and I think I've taken those qualities on board in all of my friendships as I've grown up.

That said, it was kind of my job to get involved in all the petty drama when I was on *TOWIE*. It could be cliquey too and I regret how I handled a lot of situations when I was on the show. I've always had this idea in my head that being a good friend is about being loyal, and on the show that meant ganging up against someone just because my mate had a problem with them. I still massively value loyalty in terms of being there for someone, but that doesn't mean if they're arguing with another person, you have to go at them as well. Part of loyalty is about being honest. Sometimes your mate is actually in the wrong, and it's your job to tell them that in a kind way. I've been in a lot of arguments over the years where I thought I was backing people, doing it for the right reasons and the best intentions, but then I've sat down and thought, actually my friend is the one in the fucking wrong. Now, I know that being a good friend means saying, 'Mate, I love you, but you're wrong.' I'll always stand up for my friends when they need it, but true friendship isn't just blindly following them into battle.

I've heard a lot of people in my industry say that it's hard to make and keep friends when you're 'famous'. To be honest, I find that to be bollocks and a bit of a cop-out. If you stick to your morals and values, you shouldn't find it that hard to maintain genuine friendships. I have several close mates who aren't in the public eye – both from before I was on TV and friends I've made since then. Sure, I've had some old friends reach out to me being like, 'Man, how have you been? I don't suppose you could help me get tickets for . . .' You won't believe the number of stag dos I got invited to after I went on *TOWIE*. Yeah, there are people I know who would happily name-drop me to get something they wanted. But I don't hold that against anyone. It doesn't mean they're bad people. Fuck me, we all want things from people, and fair play to them. I just know to keep those people at a reasonable distance. It doesn't mean we can't have fun together every once in a while.

I know a lot of people who say, 'I keep my circle small', like it's a badge of honour. I think it's fair enough to have an inner circle of people you really, truly trust and who feel like family. But I definitely think we should give more credit to those outer rings of people you stay in touch with but maybe don't see as often. I don't actually think it's healthy to only rely on a very small group of people – we all need different people for different things. There will be the going-out mates, who you call up when you just want to have a good time and fuck everything else.

Then there will be the people who you can just sit with on a sofa silently scrolling through your phones, knowing you don't have to perform or entertain them. That's a sign of true love. And there are the people you'll call when you're in a police cell and need to be bailed out (hypothetically speaking). Sometimes, you'll find people who are a mix of all the different qualities, and that's a very special thing. But it's also okay to draw on what different people have to offer and not expect to get everything you need from a few people.

Over the years, I've been in a lot of friendship groups and I always feel at home in group settings. I take on the role of 'Party Pete' and will definitely be the person at the bar, surrounded by people, buying shots of tequila and offering out cigarettes. Group friendships are really interesting to me, because every group has its own dynamic. There's normally some sort of hierarchy. You often have a leader – the one who organises everything, and can be a bit dominating. Then there's the villain – the one who is a bit of a dickhead, but you stay friends with them anyway. Then there's the one who is always the butt of the joke, and the one who is a bit quiet. I think it's natural for people to take on roles in groups, but the best friendships are the ones where you can change your role as you go along, everyone takes on different bits as and when needed and no one feels forced into anything. It becomes stifling when you're cast in a specific role and you're just expected to stay like that forever. I think people can outgrow friendships because of that, which is understandable. The people around you should accept you no matter what mood you're in and what role you're taking on that day. You're allowed to adapt and shift. Friendship groups should feel like a team – and everyone in the room should feel like they're part of something special. And that includes your mate's weird mate who they brought along for the evening. I hate cliquey-ness in groups. It never hurts to be kind and welcoming to people. I'd absolutely hate for anyone to feel excluded.

Alongside groups though, I think it's essential to have one-to-one friendships. It's fucking amazing to have people in your life who you can spend hours with and never get bored. And I've found some of my best mates in the most random, unexpected places. One unlikely friendship I made was when I went on a TV show called *Celebrity Island with Bear Grylls* – where we were stranded on a desert island. When I saw James Cracknell's name on the list, I thought he couldn't be more opposite to me – he's a posh multiple-gold-medallist Olympic rower – and, unsurprisingly, he had no fucking clue who I was. I thought we'd probably butt heads, but, right from day one, we became so close. I absolutely adore the geezer, and even went to his wedding. Likewise, it might surprise you to hear that I'm close with Coleen Nolan. You'd never put us together, but I bloody love the woman. I think it's so important to not be restrictive of who you think your mates 'should' be. That's all bollocks. You should be around people because you genuinely enjoy their company, not because of how it looks or what you think is right. Again, it comes back to being authentic. Who you surround yourself with says a lot about who you actually are.

I'm really lucky to have made some proper close friends in the industry, one of whom is Vicky Pattison. We met years ago because we were both booked to do a PA together in Somerset. *Geordie Shore* was massive at the time, and I was pretty new to *TOWIE*, so I was basically Vicky's assistant at the PA. Everyone fucking loved her, and they were like, 'Oh there's that other guy.' We instantly clicked because we are very similar. We both have a savage sense of humour, but we're also quite strong on our morals and values, and bonded about dogs and family and all that shit. I remember there was traffic on the way back to London, so we were stuck in the back of a cab for six hours just talking crap and having the best time.

It was such an organic, natural friendship and we always have so much fun together. I know her family and she's met my mum, which not many people have. We've both gone through those wild years together, staying up all night and then rocking up for filming in the morning without having slept, but we've also grown out of that shit too (well, at least, she has). She's so supportive and even came to watch me do *The Real Full Monty*, where I had to whack my bollocks out on stage (for charity, not just for fun). She sat in the front row and we were that close that I think I landed a bollock on her forehead, poor girl. We've worked together a lot and now even share the same management.

In the past, people I've dated have had a bit of a problem with my relationship with Vick. To be honest, I have a lot of female mates, and that has led women to become suspicious or not trust that it's all platonic. But I think it's such crap when people say men can't be friends with women, and that there's always an attraction there. Of course, sometimes that's true, and I've got myself in hot water in the past. I once lost a close friendship because we stepped over the line and couldn't come back from it. But most of my friendships with women have never had anything remotely romantic to them. They're like my sisters. I think I gravitate towards women because the most important people in my life have always been my mum and my nan. And I believe women gravitate towards me in friendships because I'm quite protective and reliable; my female mates say they feel safe with me, which can be unusual with men (which, by the way, is so fucking sad).

I've learned so much from my female friends. Friendships with women can feel more natural; there's no bravado or playing up to a character. I've already said before that I believe women are more emotionally intelligent than men, and I think us geezers can learn a lot about friendship from the women in our lives. In my experience, men are less likely to talk about serious subjects with each other, while women are more likely to open up – and I also think they're more likely to be accepting if you're in a vulnerable state. I see the way women talk to each other, and it's something men can learn from. If a girl has had a breakup, their girlfriends will all rally around them and give them a shoulder to cry on. I'm not saying men don't do that for other men, but it's a bit different. They say things like, 'You're alright mate,' and 'Stay strong.' If a girl went to her mates after a breakup and said she was fine, her mates would be like, 'No, how are you *really?* What do you need? How can we help?' If the same thing happened in a group of guys, most of the men would shrug and be like, 'He said he was fine – what else can I do?'

Again, I'm making massive generalisations here, but that's just what I've noticed. Obviously, I don't think this is the case in every friendship, but it's something I've picked up on and am always trying to change. There's no reason why it has to be that way – I think we fall into certain patterns and it's just what we're accustomed to. I think all men could benefit from having close female mates, as long as they can get past the idea that men and women will always want to shag each other. It's such an outdated perspective – and it's fucking boring, to be honest with you. And I know my girl mates have said they like having a male perspective on things too – sometimes they want someone who will cut to the chase and take the piss a bit, instead of unpicking every emotion (which can sometimes make things worse). Again, it's all about balance and taking the best qualities from the people around you.

Now, I know what you're thinking. 'Pete, you've been rambling on for ages about friendship and you've still not talked about your so-called best mate: King of the Jungle, Sam Thompson.' Well, the truth is . . . we're not actually friends. It's all a big show-mance. I actually can't stand the bloke.

Just kidding. But I do find it funny when people say that. Do you honestly think I could be around Sam – the human form of a golden retriever – as much as I am, if I didn't actually like him? It's weird that, when you're in the public eye, it even opens up your friendships to scrutiny. But that means fuck-all to me, because I know I love the guy to pieces. He's my brother, even if he is probably the most annoying person known to humanity. Our friendship has taught me so much about myself and – he's going to have a fucking field day when he reads this – I actually think he makes me a better person.

The first time I met Sam actually wasn't the first time we met, but it's the first time I *remember* meeting him, so let's start there. We were both signed up to be on *Celebs Go Dating* in 2018, a reality series that is pretty much what it says on the tin . . . celebrities go on dates. That's the concept. I've been on it several times over the years, and I have to say it's one of the funnest shows I do because I get to just hang out with my mates and date. But anyway, this was the first season I went on the show, and I met Sam on the first day of filming.

I don't think many people would put me and Sam together and think we'd end up being best friends. Obviously, our careers had similarities – we had both found fame on structured reality shows (me on *TOWIE* and him on *Made in Chelsea*) and we were both struggling to remain relevant with not a shred of talent between us. But that's basically where the similarities ended. He was a posh boy, and I was a proper East-End geezer. He was extremely enthusiastic, and I was deadpan and sarcastic. He had very limited experience with dating, and I was a seasoned pro.

The first night was a dinner party, and he came bounding up to me with an awful lot of energy. My first thought was: 'What an annoying man you are.' I could tell he was a lovely guy, but just not my cup of tea. I thought I would find him aggravating. But we spent a lot of time together doing that show and, after just a few days, he had attached himself to me like a limpet to a fucking rock. We essentially became close thanks to Sam's absolute relentlessness and persistence in not leaving me the fuck alone. It's funny that, years later, I watched him do the exact same thing with Tony Bellew live on TV when he went on *I'm A Celebrity* . . . He's the kind of person who initially appears insufferable, but he eventually wears you down and you can't help but love him. I'm not trying to encourage stalking, but somehow him bombarding me with messages, calls and whatever else got me in the end. Now I can't imagine him not being there.

From very early on, I took on a big brother role with Sam (I'm actually only a couple of years older than him, despite looking like his dad). On *Celebs Go Dating*, I tried to offer some of my advice for his shocking flirting and dating skills. To this day, he leans on me a lot when he needs advice. Most of the time, I'm all too happy to help because I like having that role. It makes me feel useful. I know Sam needs a lot of fluffing, and so I take on the position of chief fluffer, giving him that reassurance he needs. But other times I'll be like, 'I don't care whether you wear the blue T-shirt or the pink T-shirt. You're in your thirties, dress yourself, you prat.' As well as the fluffing, I think he appreciates the tough love.

But what he doesn't know, and what I refrain from telling him because he'll lose his fucking mind, is that I learn as much from him as he says he does from me. He's one of the kindest, most genuine souls I've ever met, and his optimism is infectious. I think chalk and cheese can make great friends sometimes. His weaknesses are my strengths and vice versa. I can be quite pessimistic and dry, but his energy and positivity for everything lifts me up. It's a joy to be around, and I need a bit more of that in my life. Likewise, sometimes he just needs to be told the fucking truth and have someone be a bit ruthless with him. We balance each other out.

I don't think there was one specific moment when we became best friends; it was just a natural development over time. But there was one really special time, when Sam invited me to Marbella to celebrate his thirtieth birthday. I was like, 'I don't want to spend my holidays with your posh mates in Marbella. It ain't for me.' He was gutted and insisted I come, but I was adamant I wasn't going to. Meanwhile, in the background, I told his girlfriend Zara I was coming but not to tell him, and she helped me book a hotel. He'd already been there for five days with his mates, but I flew out just for the weekend. The day I arrived, Zara was an angel and sent me the location of the restaurant they were going to, so I got there in advance and sat at the table waiting for him. When Sam saw me sitting there, he was so excited and emotional. I think that's when he realised that I loved him just as much as he loved me.

No one can get me to do things I don't want to do quite like Sam. The amount of times I have travelled two hours across London just to film something stupid for his fucking TikTok is unbelievable. I don't even have TikTok. I barely understand how it works. But often he'll call me and say he's feeling down, and I'll sigh and say, 'Do you want me to come over and we can do some stupid fucking dance for your social media then?' We're still extremely different. He doesn't go out very often, and

I'm the opposite of that. But I accept him for him, and he accepts me for me, and that's why it works so well.

Me and Sam could've easily gone our separate ways after that first series of *Celebs Go Dating*, but we just liked being around each other, and we made that choice to become family to one another. Sam's that close now that I consider him family. I get along with his parents and his sister, and probably spend more time at his house than I do my own.

It's easy to say that we work together so our friendship is financially beneficial – and of course, it is. We do great together work-wise. But what people don't see is *why* we do so well together. They don't see the numerous conversations we have that are not fucking paid. The reason we work together so much is that, if we ever have an opportunity to do so, we take it because it makes work ten times more bearable. When we started our podcast, *Staying Relevant,* I was so resistant at first because I just didn't see what the point was and why anyone would listen to it. But it's now the absolute highlight of my week because I get to hang out with Sam and talk utter shit. The fact people enjoy listening to it is a bonus.

When Sam found out he was going on *I'm A Celebrity . . .*, it was a massive thing for him as he's wanted to do it ever since he was a kid. He was so excited to be offered it, but he was also really nervous. He'd recently been diagnosed with attention deficit hyperactivity disorder (ADHD) and autism, which explains why he's often struggled with new people, and big groups can cause him a lot of anxiety. He wasn't sure how he would feel and how he'd be received by his camp mates and the public. We spent an awful long time before he went in discussing his worries – he was overthinking all sorts. But I kept saying to him: 'Just go in there and be you. Don't be anything you're not. Enjoy it. It's once in a lifetime.'

I was so proud that he did exactly that. When he knew he was going on the show, we weren't sure if Zara would still be on *Strictly Come Dancing*, so he asked if I could be the person to go out to Australia and support him. I really didn't fucking want to – but it's Sam, so I couldn't say no. I knew how much he leans on me in times of crisis, and he felt that me being there would give him a boost if he needed it. He knows he doesn't need to pretend to be strong around me. So I flew out to Australia as one of the loved ones – it was basically all wives and partners . . . and me. I think a lot of people were shocked that he would ask for a mate to come out and be his plus-one. Our friendship took people by surprise. But I also think it captured the hearts of a lot of people – because why can't men be unconditionally there for each other? Why can't men rely on their mates as their support systems, even when they have a partner and family and whatever else?

I went into the jungle to see Sam, a few days before the final, and the clip went viral on social media. I actually didn't expect it to be as emotional as it was. I thought he would be the high-energy puppy dog he usually is, but, as soon as I saw him, I could tell he was drained. When he saw me, he broke down. I think it's because I was a piece of home that was separate from the pressure of the jungle. Seeing how emotional he was, it made me emotional too. I told him to just keep going, to keep being himself and that I was proud of him. It was all true. I knew he would do the same for me if I needed it. And then, a few days later, I met him again on the infamous *I'm A Celebrity* . . . bridge when he was crowned King of the Jungle. I was so fucking happy and excited for him, even though my face had blown up to the size of a melon thanks to an infected mosquito bite. Fucking typical.

It was amazing reading some of the messages I received after that. People were saying they're so glad their sons could see the importance of platonic male friendships. It's odd that our silly little friendship could be inspirational for people, but I'm really proud of that – because it's true that it's not something you see often. On the other side of the coin, there were people saying our relationship is weird. I guess it's because society has constantly told men to 'man up'. Men aren't taught how to support each other and be genuine friends, or they're taught to feel a bit weird if they do. But men are just as entitled to close friendships as women are. And if you don't appreciate the love you have for your mates, you're missing out on such a beautiful part of life.

As men, I think it's extra-important to nurture our friendships with our mates and be vulnerable. Male suicide rates are through the roof, and it's well-known that a big reason for that is that men don't feel like they can open up and talk about their feelings. It's not about forcing people to talk because I know first-hand that it can be hard to put all your shit on the table. When you feel backed into a corner, it can just put your guard up even more. But it's about checking in and saying, 'I'm here whenever you want to talk. Whatever you need, I can help. I've got you.' I would drop everything to support a mate, but I'm not always the best at checking in with them because I'll assume that, if they're not reaching out, they're all good and they don't need anything. That's not necessarily the right way of doing things though and I know this in the reverse from when I am at my lowest. Often, we don't want to be burdens to our friends so we just suffer in silence. But if someone reached out to you, you might go, 'Actually, you know what, I'm not really fine.' So I'm trying to do that more. Being a friend means not excusing yourself from hard conversations.

There are lots of ways you can encourage friends to open up without forcing them. I find that, with Sam, if I open up about something that's going on in my own life, he's more likely to tell me how he's feeling. It's a good way in. If you tell them you've had a shitty day, they might go, 'Tell me about it,' and then also get something off their chest. The more you can be vulnerable, the more you give other people space to be vulnerable too.

And I can't stress this enough: if someone is brave enough to open up to you, don't be a fucking dickhead and downplay how they're feeling. Some people have the tendency to do this, don't they? They'll say things like, 'Well, it's not as bad as X,' or 'Just imagine how I feel going through Y.' Every feeling is valid and it is all relative – it's not the trauma Olympics. You shouldn't need to compete with your friends. Even if their problem seems like nothing to you, you don't need to form an opinion on it. Your job as a mate is to listen and be there. The more you make someone feel bad about opening up, the less likely they'll do it again in future.

I've never been very good at romantic relationships (more on that in the next chapter), but friendships require a lot of the same skills. You have to be patient and understanding. You have to make an effort. Yes, we all get busy and life gets in the way, but if you really value your friend, you shouldn't leave them on 'read' for days on end (something I'm trying to get better at). Obviously, friendships are lower maintenance in that you're not expected to be at your mates' beck and call every minute of every day (although tell that to Sam), but they do still need communication, even if that communication is every few months, and you can meet up just once a year and feel like nothing has changed. The best friendships can survive a bit of space (again, Sam needs to hear this), but you still have to put the work in to make sure they don't disappear altogether. It's about the quality of the time you spend together, not necessarily the quantity. Of course, it's nice to have friends who live on the same road as you and you can see them every fucking day. But that's not the reality for most people – not everyone has a set-up like the TV show *Friends*, and I think that can make people feel like their friendships aren't as strong. But that's bollocks. If you have people in your life who are loyal and reliable, and respect you just as much as you respect them, that's incredible – even if it is hard to align your schedules to meet up.

Like everything in life, friendships can't be rainbows and butterflies all the time. It's just not realistic, is it? As with romantic relationships, it's okay to have conflict every once in a while, but it's about how you handle disagreements. Me and Sam disagree all the time. We come from different backgrounds and have different outlooks on life, so it's unsurprising. It can get quite heated, but, at the end of it all, we'll just be like, 'Fuck it, let's agree to disagree, I'll see you tomorrow.'

One of the hurdles people have in friendships is that we expect others to be perfect people. We think our mates should know exactly what we're feeling all the time, what we need and how to look out for us. The reality is that everyone has their own shit going on and nobody is perfect. Everyone has their flaws. And if you're always upset with your mates about their flaws, you're basically suggesting you're a perfect person yourself (I don't know you, but I can guarantee you're not). Obviously, if a friendship is consistently causing you agg and making you upset, only you know what's best for you – and if you need to distance yourself from that person, you should do that. And of course, there are absolutely sackable offences in a friendship, like if someone has betrayed your trust. If you can't trust someone, any kind of relationship is dead in the water (the same goes for romantic relationships and family members too).

But I think there's way too much conversation these days about just cutting 'toxic' people out of your life. Again, it's this trend of removing anyone or anything from your life that poses some kind of challenge. I don't think that's right. Overall, your friends should lift you up and make you feel good, yes. But it's also okay to be like, 'They're going through a rough time right now, so I'm going to let that snarky comment slide.' Or, 'They're being flaky at the moment, so I'm going to lower my expectations of them.' Allow people to be human and fuck up a bit. Life isn't perfect and neither are our friends. Accept that.

Too many people are afraid to admit they're wrong or say 'sorry'. I think 'sorry' is a dirty word for a lot of men because it implies weakness. Being stubborn and digging your heels in is seen as a show of strength, which I have been guilty of. Look up 'stubborn' in the dictionary, and you'll find my miserable face next to it. I take full accountability for that. But I'm also self-aware enough to know I've been wrong in a lot of situations. My nan always taught me that, if you're in the wrong, apologise. There's no fucking shame in it. If you can put yourself into other people's shoes and take responsibility for your own actions, it will help your friendships. Trust me, it's worth it.

At the end of the day, you shouldn't lose sight of why we all want friends to begin with. We need other people for the fun and energy they bring into our lives. As kids, we gravitate towards the people we find fun and who make us feel happy, and the same goes for adult friendships. When all is said and done, our pals should be a positive influence on us. We should enjoy the time we spend with them. We should like who we are around them. We should insist they do a shot of Baby Guinness even though they swore they were leaving two hours ago (I'm sort of joking, and sort of not – your friends should respect your boundaries, but I think real friends also know when you *actually* do want to stay for another round). It's okay if you have some friends who are only there for the fun times, but are nowhere to be seen when shit hits the fan. Those people have their place too. It's just that the closest friendships are the ones that can survive both.

If you're reading this and thinking, 'Fuck, I don't have those kinds of friends I can rely on,' the first thing I would say is, you probably do. There will be someone in your life who thinks you're the fucking bollocks, who would be more than happy to help you out in your time of need. Maybe you just don't see it that way and you haven't given them a shot. My advice is just to reach out. Open up the conversation, make an effort, get vulnerable. It won't hurt to try. And if you're really struggling with feeling supported by the people in your life, it's never too late to make new friends. I've picked up new mates at every stage of my life and from all different age brackets. There's no shame in being best mates with the old dear who lives down the road; if that's who you get along with, happy days. You can find people you'll connect with in the most unlikely places. You just have to be willing to look.

You can be a friend to anyone, even if it's a stranger on the street. You're not friends with someone just because you know the name of their pet or you've met their sibling. That's knowledge, it's not friendship. Friendship is being able to offer someone something they need – whether you're giving them a laugh or a shoulder to cry on. A friend should make you feel better, even if it's for a glimmering fucking second. In the end, it all comes back to kindness. Indiscriminate acts of kindness – that's friendship.

I feel really blessed that I have so many people in my life who always show me kindness when I need it, but sometimes I struggle to receive it. As I've said, my nan was my best friend and, when she died, I had never felt so lonely. It felt like I had lost everything and that no one would understand what I was going through. I didn't expect my friends to be there for me, because

I never really expect anything from anyone. But they were. Vick would send me regular messages, saying, 'I know you don't want to talk right now, but I'm here.' Sam would invite me round on Christmas and birthdays, even though I wanted to hibernate, because he hated the idea of me being on my own. I have the kind of friends who would bang my door down just to let me know they're waiting outside. Because I'm me, and I hate being a burden, I've struggled to let that love in and believe it's real.

It's easier for me to believe that no one really wants to see me down, even when my mates have consistently proven otherwise. I tell myself that my friends only stick around for 'Party Pete' and not 'Crying-On-The-Sofa Pete'. That guy is no fun at all – even I fucking hate the bloke. When I'm sad, I find it easier to sur-round myself with acquaintances who don't really know me. It offers more of a distraction because the people who know me well can tell when I'm not doing good. Sometimes that's con-fronting – I don't always want one of my close friends looking into my soul and asking me deep questions. In a way, that makes me a bad friend because I'm not listening to people when they say they love me. We all deserve respect, and I should know that I deserve just as much as I give to other people. Friendship is a two-way street and people want to be able to support me and they want to be there. Part of being a good friend is being able to receive friendship. It's about recognising all the love in your life. I'm working on that.

I'll probably always be a lone wolf, to a certain degree. I'll always want to retreat into my own reclusive Pete den and shut everyone else out when times are hard. But I'm getting better at pulling my walls down for the people who really matter to me. We can all feel lonely sometimes, even if we seem like the life and soul of the party and we're constantly surrounded by people. I'm not ashamed to admit that. We don't talk about loneliness enough. When we do, we think of some little old man who has no one to come and visit him. But everyone can be lonely, and it's on us to change that – both by reaching out to help others and allowing other people to help us. At the end of the day, we're social creatures. We need each other.

Final Fucking Thoughts: Even lone wolves need company

★ We should all have friends who come from different age brackets, genders and backgrounds. It makes life a lot more interesting.

★ Opposites attract. You don't need to have a lot in common with your mates; sometimes it works even better when you balance each other out.

★ Being a good friend isn't just about being there for other people. It's also about allowing people to be there for you.

CHAPTER 6

Love Should Be Easy . . .
But It Usually Ain't

I t's safe to say I have dated a lot of people in my time, and I'm not one for long-term relationships. The longest one I've been in was about eighteen months, and even that was on-and-off. But it's not because I find it fun to jump from one relationship to another (although, admittedly, this was the case when I was younger). The reason I can't settle into a relationship now is that I've fallen into a pattern of being alone. I'm out a lot, working, constantly socialising and dating, but, when all is said and done, my sanctuary is just me, on my own, with my dogs. I don't really know any other way to be.

Most of us have difficulties navigating romantic relationships. Even people who appear to be in the happiest, healthiest marriages will have their own problems, even if everything looks perfect from the outside. Maybe you're a serial monogamist and you jump from one romance to the next because you just hate the idea of being alone. Maybe you're unhappy in a long-term relationship and you feel resentful about everything you've had to give up. Or maybe, like me, you're an eternally single grumpy old man, who actually craves love and affection, but doesn't quite know how to get there.

The problem is, I grew up surrounded by broken relationships. You already know about my mum and dad's messy divorce. My mum's new fella had divorced too. My granddad wasn't my real granddad (I heard the stories of how badly my nan's ex had hurt her before I was born, and they stuck with me). I saw how much unhealthy relationships had broken people and I knew I didn't want to go down that path. I didn't want to be in a relationship unless it was perfect. In a weird way, I think all the fucked-up relationships around me gave me a really idealised fairy-tale view of what a relationship should be. I've always believed that the right relationship should just magically work, ignoring the fact you have to put the effort in, compromise and navigate difficult times. I viewed relationships in extremes: they were either shiny and perfect, or completely fucked. In my eyes, there was no in between.

It comes back to that t-word again: trauma. When you think about relationship traumas, you probably think about your own past relationships – the ones that were toxic or failed, or the ones that made you feel awful or guilty. But you don't just carry your own, you also carry what you've seen. The relationships we see growing up are all we know and, sadly, they impact how we operate in relationships when we're older. They are the blueprint. If you have parents and grandparents who have been together for fifty-odd years, you'll know it's not easy, but you'll also probably know it's worth sticking with. Whereas if you see people walk away from things, you'll assume that's the normal thing to do.

It can go either way, can't it? We either repeat the patterns we've seen or we do what we can to not repeat those same stories from our parents and grandparents. I think I've gone so far out of my way not to repeat their mistakes that I've ended up making plenty more on my own. That said, I obviously don't blame my family's relationships for my own failings. I take responsibility for my own actions and patterns. But I think it's interesting to look at your personal background to see how it has impacted you.

I have always been quite confident at dating, meaning I became known as a player fairly early on in my life. If I went out with my mates, there was always this sense of bravado and admiration; they'd say, 'You can count on Pete to pick up a bird.' It was almost like a badge of honour and something to be proud of, as horrible as that sounds. I won't lie, the culture was toxic as fuck back then. Being known for getting with women was a sign of respect from your peers. I'm not proud to say that, but it was a big part of male camaraderie, especially in my circles. To be honest, though there's more awareness now about how misogynistic and unacceptable that is, it's still like that in many ways, but it's just masked. It was like viewing women as prizes to impress your mates. I never saw it like that though, at least not consciously. I felt like I was having a good time, whoever I was dating was having a good time and everyone was happy – happy days. But I can't deny the role that this culture probably had on my mindset.

I can't lie to you: I really enjoy dating because I genuinely enjoy meeting new people. I've already mentioned how much I want everyone around me to have a good time, and the same applies to dating. From my perspective, I've never had a bad date and that's because I love chatting and finding out about someone. People think I have go-to moves for picking up women, but I promise I don't. It's a lot simpler than people would think. I just make eye contact, ask questions and listen, and I try not to talk at someone as if I'm selling myself. To be honest, these are basic things for any conversation with anyone. Just making an effort to get to know someone and being really open to having an interesting conversation will help you form deeper connections – whether they're romantic or platonic.

There's a lot of validation that comes from dating too, because it's so nice to feel wanted. I believe everyone wants other people to want them, but most people just aren't honest about it. You might say you don't care, but you do. It's human nature to enjoy that feeling. Likewise, if your friend was getting all the attention on a night out, you'd think, 'Why am I not getting that?' If someone says they don't care about this stuff, they're fucking lying. We all have pride and egos and fragile self-esteem that need fluffing as often as possible. I don't think there's anything wrong with that. We should be more honest about it.

It's probably no surprise to you that I hate dating apps. I'm an old-fashioned geezer at the end of the day; I much prefer meeting people in person. I find the apps kind of soulless, and think it's really hard to tell what someone's like from their pictures and their answers to silly questions. The only way you can really tell if you are attracted to someone is if you meet them and speak to them in person. It's not just that edited pictures can be misleading (although that too), but sometimes a person who isn't the most conventionally attractive can be extremely sexy. In the same way, the most textbook-beautiful person can have the sex appeal of a metal rod. I think sexiness comes down to presence. You can't really put your finger on it – and it's all too easy to judge someone off a picture when you actually have no idea how interesting and sexy they are. It's all about how someone makes you feel, how captivating they are. Sometimes you can speak to someone and feel like there's no one else in the fucking room. The problem with dating apps is you can't get a sense of that shit at all over a screen. It's far too manufactured.

I see why apps can be useful though, especially if you're not the kind of person who feels confident enough approaching someone at a bar or in a cafe. It wouldn't be fair for me to completely slag them off, given I know lots of couples who met on dating apps and have great relationships. But the thing about constantly swiping left and right, is it gives you the idea that there are always plenty more fish in the sea and you can keep swiping until you find that perfect person. Back in the day, you'd meet someone and think they're alright, then get married and have loads of babies and that would be it, by and large. I'm not saying that was a good thing by any means, but one problem with our modern times is that we've all become really fussy. One tiny flaw and we think, 'Ah well, I'll just find someone better.'

It means that people say they have the 'ick' when someone they're dating does something really normal, like lick their spoon or wear a pair of ugly shoes. I fucking hate 'ick' culture. If you're not familiar, an 'ick' is essentially a small thing that someone does to disgust you, that makes the relationship (whether romantic or platonic) irredeemable. And no, it's not just because it's a term often used to describe my Instagram captions, and because I have at one point been nicknamed 'Pete Icks'. I personally think icks just don't exist. When applied to relationships, an ick is just an excuse to cut and run. If you really liked someone, you wouldn't find them running across the road for a fucking bus disgusting and enough of a red flag to bin them off (yes, someone told me once that this was a genuine ick for them). Icks are just quirks. They're unimportant in the grand scheme of things. And if you really liked someone enough, you wouldn't notice them at all.

I get it. Talking about your 'icks' is often just banter, and I'm on board with that (even if I'm the butt of the joke). But I do think the fascination we all have with icks speaks to a wider problem with modern dating. It's just picking apart people's flaws, ain't it? The problem is, so many of us believe that, a) the perfect person exists, b) that we are perfect ourselves, and c) that we deserve perfection. Look, I've been guilty of this too. I think it's normal to have high expectations. But when we focus so much on what we don't want, we lose sight of what we do want and what actually matters.

In the same vein, I know so many people who are obsessed with having a 'type' (no thanks to *Love Island* for making this even more of a thing). Your 'type' is usually a way of describing your ideal partner, looks-wise: 'tall, dark and handsome' is a classic one. But it can also include their job, whether they have pets or any other tick-box requirements. I think that's all absolute bollocks. Again, it's just another judgemental way to pick people apart – and it perpetuates the idea that the perfect person actually exists 'on paper'. I used to think I had a specific type, but I'm a lot more open-minded now. I realised that only going after a certain 'type' of person was cutting me off from people I'd connect better with. It's so limiting, and often it's based on an idea of what we think we should find attractive, rather than qualities we actually find attractive. I still think looks are important because you need that sexual spark to build a relationship, but I put far less emphasis on appearance now than I did when I was younger, when everything was about getting with the hottest girl. A fun personality and good morals are much more important to me now.

And here's where my hypocrisy comes back in full swing – I know that we place too much emphasis on perfection in dating and that big connection right from the start. I know that the perfect relationship and the perfect person don't exist. And yet, I'm still holding on to the fairy tale. I push people away when I notice the slightest signs that we're not suited or it might not work. I think it doesn't always matter how much understanding of a situation we have; we can have all the gear and still no idea about how to put those lessons into action. We still play out our traumas and repeat our patterns all the fucking time.

I would never blame 'fame' for my relationship issues, but I don't think the life I lead has particularly helped. When I appeared in the limelight, I became a 'player' not just to my mates and the people who knew me, but to seemingly everyone I met. What started off as a proud identity ended up becoming a disease. The fuckboy persona became a self-fulfilling prophecy. If I dated someone for more than a few weeks, it would go something like this: boy meets girl, boy has to prove he's not an arsehole, girl finally accepts boy and trusts him, then boy ends up actually being an arsehole.

Trying to have a relationship in the public eye is hard, and I take my hat off to anyone who's able to do it. The speculation can be overwhelming sometimes. If I had a pound for every time I'd been 'linked to' someone in the press, I'd be a millionaire. Most of the time, the women I'm pictured with are my friends; one time, it was even my mum. Even though I'm pictured with women all the time, I'm actually very private about my dating life. Since my reality TV years, the public hasn't really known about my most important relationships. Half of the stuff I see about myself isn't actually true. It's the same rhetoric over and over. We all evolve, learn, get better and do things differently, but the playboy persona follows me around. I feel like I'm not really given the space to change. Because when you're told something enough, you start believing it. It's hard to rise above all that and be like, 'I don't have to be what they say I am.' Same goes for everyone – it doesn't matter if you're in the public eye or not. If you're constantly told you're stupid, you'll believe you're stupid. If you're constantly told you're an arsehole, you'll be an arsehole. I'm constantly told that I'm incapable of being in a relationship, and it has become true. It doesn't have to be true though. I'm the master of my own destiny. But it doesn't always feel that way.

I think part of the reason the press has such a field day with me is that my bachelor lifestyle is still frowned upon in wider society. We have this idea of what makes a 'good person' – and that's usually someone who is married with a family. Dating lots of people and shagging around has always been seen as morally 'bad'. It has been that way for fucking centuries. Even in this day and age, it's hard to shake. I can't complain too much, because I know women have it a lot worse. I've seen it with my female friends in the public eye, who have been absolutely roasted for dating around – they've been called 'slags' and all the rest of it. It's awful. I know I haven't had it as bad, but those expectations and ideals are still there.

The problem is, I reckon our society makes a lot of people settle down with someone who isn't necessarily the right person for them because they think that's the 'right' thing to do. We all feel a huge amount of pressure when it comes to relationships. For me, that includes the newspapers, but I'm also talking about parents, friends and all those knobs from your childhood who you don't talk to anymore but still follow on Instagram. It's easier to let all the outside noise determine your life and relationships, and think, 'Well everyone's getting married and having kids so I should probably do that.' Again, it can take courage to break away from these norms and do what's right for you.

That said, I have the opposite problem. 'Settling down' is the bit I just can't do. The minute a relationship gets to the point where I seem to be having an impact on someone's life, it scares the shit out of me. Because if I can have a positive impact on a person's life, that means I can also have a negative impact. I hate the idea of hurting people and I always want to impact people's lives in a positive way. So, as soon as there becomes a possibility that I could fuck up and hurt them, I leg it – because I'd rather have no impact on someone than be the one to break their heart. In reality, I often do it too late, when the damage is already done. By being so scared of hurting someone, I end up hurting them anyway, and I hurt myself too.

I've always taken pride in how much I respect other people. It's important to me to treat people well. That's how my mum and nan raised me. I always think, 'I do nice things for people.' If I'm dating a woman, I'll take them to fancy places and give them compliments and support them with whatever they've got going on in their life. But all that stuff isn't necessarily treating someone well. If you don't listen and respect someone for having their own thoughts and feelings, that is treating someone badly. I've had women say, 'I love you' to me, and I've point-blank said, 'No you don't.' That's because I didn't believe it. I've always thought I was unloveable. But still, how fucking out of order is that? Who am I to tell someone how they feel?

I'm completely aware that this is a pattern I have, and it stems from the fact I don't think I'm ever enough. I believe women have loved the idea of me, but not actually the real me. It comes back to what we spoke about in Chapter 3: we know too much about ourselves, and that's why so many of us struggle with poor self-worth. I sometimes think of myself as the worst person on the planet because I know about all the bad shit and it out-weighs the good. For someone who views himself as confident (and is probably viewed this way by others), I'm actually very insecure. I think the same goes for every other arrogant prick in your life. More often than not, it's a facade.

So often, the issues we have in relationships come back to how we view ourselves. I've seen it time and time again. Like the bloke who was always called 'ugly' in school, so he clings on to the only woman he thinks will ever love him and ignores all the red flags. Or the woman who has been in so many toxic, horrible relationships that she thinks it's all she deserves. We all do it. Sure, relationships can be messy by themselves, but we bring all of our own mess into them as well. So then, you end up with a massive pile of crap you have to wade through.

There's a bigger question here: how the fuck do you get into relationships without hurting people or being hurt? I don't think there's actually an answer to that, though. We just don't know what the future holds. At the end of the day, love and relationships are a leap of faith. I admire people who are able to say, 'Yes, that's my person,' and just decide to give it their all. You can't control the future and you'll never know if that choice was worth it, but you make the choice anyway. I think that's fucking beautiful, and brave.

So maybe I'm just at stage one: the awareness stage. At least I recognise my patterns and know where I'm going wrong. There are lots of resources out there to help you on your journey to self-reflection. When I started writing this chapter, my editor forced me to do an online quiz about what my 'attachment style' is. It comes from theories developed by psychologists in the sixties and seventies, and it's all about your ability to feel loved and protected – and a lot of it comes from childhood. There are three main attachment styles: secure, anxious and avoidant (although there are sub-groups too), and they're all pretty self-explanatory. Any guesses which one I am?

You're probably thinking, 'Pete, you didn't need to do a stupid quiz. It's obvious you're avoidant.' And while that's true, doing it did reveal some interesting insights. It also felt quite good to know I'm not the only fucker who acts the way I do, and there are other people out there with the same commitment phobias. In a way, it was nice to read the description that this can come from trauma (undoubtedly, feeling unloved and left behind as a kid) and not just because there's something terribly wrong with me. It made me feel like this shit isn't necessarily my fault, and it gave me hope that I can change one day.

Now we come to the part of the chapter where I share my advice about navigating romantic relationships. Here's my biggest one: don't be like me. My love life is a car crash. Learn from all the things I've got wrong. One of which is poor communication. I have a tendency to internalise my fears and doubts. It's easy to do. You create stories in your head about what a relationship is or isn't, which become completely detached from reality. But if you don't verbalise this with your partner and keep them involved with what's going on in your head, it will be your biggest downfall. We all make assumptions all the time. We assume other people can read our minds. We assume they're thinking something that they're really not. We assume they feel a certain way, and we don't give them a chance to tell us otherwise. You'll know the saying: 'Don't assume, because it makes an ASS out of U and ME.' It's true. You can avoid making incorrect assumptions by communicating, and then really listening. Ask the tough questions. Listen to the answers. Express how you feel in a given moment – don't wait until it all piles up and feels too overwhelming to address. It takes courage to open up, but it's so rewarding.

That said, you have to accept that other people aren't necessarily the same as you. They might not have the same style of communication. I don't advocate for word-vomiting all your bizarre thoughts and feelings as soon as they come up, as that can be shitty for your partner too. I think you have to make an effort to understand the person you're dating and how best to deliver information or work through things with them. It's a bit of a dance, being in a relationship. You have to take the right steps at the right time and it requires both of you giving each other a bit of room to freestyle, while also being in sync.

How you actually achieve the perfect dance is beyond me, but maybe that's the whole point: relationships can't be perfect. Those fairy tales we believed in when we were younger? We've been fed a lie. I still think you can be soulmates with someone, but it's never going to be rosy 100 per cent of the time. Good relationships require a fuck-ton of compromise. You have to acknowledge your differences and embrace them. You can't always do things your way; you have to find a way to meet in the middle. This is something I'm not great at, as you probably know by now.

It's also about letting go of the idea of 'perfect'. Absolutely no one is perfect and, if you think someone is, you're putting them on a pedestal, which can be unhealthy in itself. It means they have further to fall. We all fuck up; we can all be a giant ick (yes, even you). We all have annoying tendencies, like how we stack the dishwasher or the annoying phrases we say on a daily basis. That's called being human. We can't expect other people to be perfect, and we also shouldn't expect it of ourselves. And we absolutely can't expect relationships to be perfect either.

You also can't expect a person to fix you. Sorry to break it to ya, but a romantic relationship won't magically solve all your problems and save you from your insecurities and traumas. That's not how life works. You have to do the majority of the donkey work yourself, rather than waiting for someone else to come and do it for you. The thing is, when you get into a relationship, you're intertwining two different people's thoughts, feelings, goals and whatever else. It's a whole mismatch of right and wrong and contradiction. You have to understand yourself and another person at the same time, which doubles the complexity. So the more you can deal with your own shit and make that a priority, the easier you'll find navigating life with another person. And anyway, a relationship shouldn't complete you – I don't think it should be the be-all and end-all. You should always be an independent human at the end of the day. A good relationship shouldn't become your whole life, but it should make it better.

In the same way, we often think we can fix another person. Believe me when I say this: no one is going to fix me. It has to come from me, no one else. The same applies to everyone. You either want to change and you're doing that work, or you don't and you ain't. We spend far too much time thinking we can change other people. We can have an impact on people, yes. I've been in plenty of relationships with women who have undoubtedly made me a better person. But I'm still not happy in my core. That ain't anyone else's fault. That's on me, and me alone.

If you're considering ending a relationship, I think you have to differentiate between whether a relationship is unhappy or you're just in an unhappy moment right now. It can be hard to remember the good times when you're in the tunnel of a bad time. If you're really not happy in a relationship, you should leave it. If you're not happy in your life right now, you should fix it. But it can be really hard to tell the difference, and it's something I have struggled with throughout my dating life. I think you need to accept the other person for who they are, but you also have to know your limit for acceptance. It's good to have strong boundaries and know what is and isn't worth your time. All relationships have bad times, but there should always be a much higher ratio of good to bad. A lot of it comes down to emotional intelligence. You need to have your own top shelf in order before you can make that judgement call.

And if you're going through a breakup, the best advice I can give is to process it your way. Don't let any other fucker tell you how you should be feeling or experiencing it. I think you have to give yourself time to process it, because it's like grief, ain't it? We're not pieces of elastic. You can't necessarily snap back to the person you were before that person impacted your life. I think a lot of people try to do this, and it bites them in the arse later down the line. Take your time. And try to remember that there were lessons from that relationship – whether it was good or bad. Every relationship, whether it works or doesn't work, was worth something. Every experience is a learning curve, so try not to look back and regret. Instead, think of all the mistakes you can try to leave behind and all the positives you can take forward into your life and your next relationships.

I know that the love I lack in romantic relationships, I make up for with my family, friends and dogs. There can be romance in every connection you have in your life, even the platonic ones. I think we've lost sight of what 'romance' actually means. It's not a bunch of roses or sexy lingerie. I think romance is the small shit we do for each other – selfless acts of love that we do just because we really care about someone. We don't do it to make a statement or have something to post on Instagram, we just do it because it feels natural and easy. Romance is squeezing someone's hand and saying, 'It's going to be alright.' It's texting someone to check in on a difficult anniversary. It's meeting someone at the train station to walk them home. When you look at romance that way, I have plenty of it in my life. I'm sure you do too – whatever your relationship status.

Final Fucking Thoughts: Love should be easy . . . but it usually ain't

- ★ Life ain't perfect, so we can't expect romantic relationships to be perfect either.
- ★ You'll never be able to fix someone else, and a romantic partner ain't going to fix you. A relationship will never solve all your problems.
- ★ You'll only improve your romantic relationships when you can identify your patterns and mistakes.

CHAPTER 7

Short-Term Solutions Don't
Fix Long-Term Problems

I've already said it countless times in this book: life can be a
pile of shit. And because of that, we all have things we lean
on every day to make it a bit more bearable and get the best out
of it. Some of those things are healthy – like seeing friends, exer-
cising and getting a good amount of sleep. And some things are
unhealthy – like drinking, smoking, overworking, putting yourself in harm's way and just generally being a self-destructing
mess. Any guesses as to which ones I do?

Once again, I'm not here to preach, because I know that a lot
of my usual habits aren't good for me, but I still do most of them,
and it's unlikely that I'm going to stop any of them altogether, to
be completely honest with you. The reality is that I use things
like alcohol and work as coping mechanisms when I am stressed
or sad, to distract myself from dealing with my emotions. And
don't look at me and judge me because I know you do the same
thing. Except maybe not the exact same thing; your coping
mechanisms might be different to mine. Perhaps you spend
money you don't have shopping online or you binge-watch a
Netflix series without even coming up for breath. I think the first

step is recognising that these things aren't necessarily helping you out, as much as they feel good in the moment. The second step – actually making changes – is the trickier bit, because we get so accustomed to our habits that they become part of who we are. We rely on them. They become our safety nets.

Something I'm known for is that I love a drink. On my podcast, one of my opening lines is: 'I will be drinking and, if you don't like that, go fuck yourself.' I think if any of my mates had to draw a picture of me from memory, they'd sketch me holding a pint of Guinness or a shot of tequila. Sam always jokes that, if he can't find me at an event, he'll just go to the bar. I might as well be a bar stool at this point, given the amount of time I spend propped up against them. I'm like a fucking homing pigeon; I always end up at the nearest establishment that serves booze.

I don't remember the first time I had a drink, but I do remember the first time I got absolutely obliterated. I was around twelve years old, while on holiday in Portugal with my mum, her fella and his kids, who are around the same age as me. Me and one of his sons stole some of the adults' red wine and got absolutely hammered. They had all gone to bed and we decided it would be hilarious to go skinny-dipping in the villa pool, causing a fucking scene, before throwing up red wine all over the house. It was an absolute mess.

Like most British kids, and particularly boys, I started on the booze young – so I got most of those really ridiculous, sloppy drunken nights out of the way early on. Because I had older friends when I was in school, I was in the pubs and clubs a lot (sometimes with a fake ID, sometimes not – it wasn't as strict back then, you see). I'm now in my mid-thirties and I've been out drinking many times since then. I never got hangovers, until the age of thirty-two – and now they hurt me. But, thankfully, they don't stop me from getting on with life. I'm not the kind of prick who gets all dramatic when my head hurts the next day and says, 'I'm never drinking again.' I hate it when people do that because we all know you will.

I'm sure you know those people who go absolutely off the rails when they get pissed. They get aggressive or overly emotional or they fall all over the place and cause chaos. This kind of behaviour makes people sit up and go, 'Hold on, that person has a problem.' My issue is that I'm actually better when I've had a drink. It softens my edges. I've already said I'm an angry person, and I can still be angry when I've had a drink, but I don't think it fuels it – it mutes it. This will sound fucking weird, but alcohol steadies me (yes, alcohol, which renders most people unable to walk in a straight line). I have spent an obscene amount of money on alcohol over the years. I want to make sure everyone is having a good time, so I foot the bill (there's 'Daddy Pete' again), but rarely drink past the point of knowing what's going on.

Of course, there have been times when I've taken it too far. But no one looks after me; I look after myself. If I feel a bit drunk, I do this thing called the 'back door exit' where I just quietly remove myself from the situation and take myself home. Sensible really. I'm like a cat going off to die slowly on my own (except, obviously, I come back to life eventually). It's not that I'm always completely in control, I'm not. It's just that no one ever sees me when I'm in a state.

Over the years, I've done some silly things thanks to alcohol. There was one night I got so drunk I decided I just wanted to go on holiday. So I got a taxi straight to the airport from the bar. My plan was to get on the next flight – I didn't even care where the fuck it was going. It was a bit of a dream of mine to do that . . . and it still is. There's something quite cool and spontaneous about it. But then I got to the airport and realised I didn't have my passport or wallet, so I got a taxi home and, by the time I got back, I was like, 'I can't be arsed,' and fell asleep. So that was a waste of time. At least if I'd actually gone somewhere it would've been a better fucking story.

On another occasion, when I was working in the City, I'd already been drinking all day and was going to join my mates in a club in town. I stopped off at a cash machine at Piccadilly Circus to get some money out, having had a lot of wine by this point, when I struck up a conversation with a homeless guy. I've always had a real affinity with the homeless; I have a lot of time for them. Maybe it's because they're perceived as outsiders and I've always felt like a bit of an outsider too. So I started chatting to this guy and he was so lovely, and offered me a can of Stella. I took the can and sat with him for a while drinking. My friends were messaging me like, 'Where the fuck are you?' But I really liked this guy and didn't want to leave him, so I asked him, 'Do you want to come out?' At first he was so confused, but he agreed to come. It was November and it was really fucking cold, so I gave the guy my suit jacket to warm him up for the walk there. We got inside the club to meet the boys, and they were like, 'Who the fuck is that?' and I was like, 'Oh I just met him outside,' not realising how strange that was. They were like, 'Is he homeless?' Look it's not his fault, but he wasn't the best-smelling bloke, so it was pretty obvious the man didn't have access to a shower. But he was really kind, so I wanted him to have a good night. Then again, he'd only been in there for fifteen minutes before stealing a bottle of vodka from the table, and my jacket, and running away. It was a nightmare as it was a three-piece suit, so now I just have the trousers and waistcoat. I've spent the last twelve years trying to find him to get that fucking jacket back. Turns out he was a bit of a dickhead after all.

If you asked me why I've enjoyed drinking so much, I'd find it difficult to answer. I always think I enjoy it in the moment, but, sometimes, when I look back on these drunken nights, in the cold light of day, I think: did I actually enjoy it? Was that really what I wanted? Or do I just drink because it's the easy option, because it's the role I have somehow fallen into? Drinking is the kind of thing that always feels like a good idea in the moment, but the hangover can be brutal – and I don't just mean physically. I'm not the kind of person who gets massive 'hangxiety' – like I said, I know myself enough to remove myself from a situation if I'm making a tit out of myself. That said, the aftermath still isn't great. When you pick up a drink, you might forget about your worries. But when you sober up, they'll hit you twice as hard.

I know a lot of people say they use alcohol as a social crutch, to make them more confident and whatnot. I'm not quite like that – I've already got a personality so I don't need alcohol to give me one. I think maybe it does help me tolerate other people, though, which is quite worrying, to be honest. But for some people alcohol can be a bonding experience. People release their inhibitions a bit when having a drink. They become less guarded. And for people who struggle to drop their walls down in normal times, it gives them an opportunity to express themselves in an authentic way, because they're not overthinking and self-editing.

The thing is, drinking is so fucking engrained in UK culture. It's the most normal thing in the world. I mean, are you really British if you didn't go down the pub with a fake ID as soon as your balls dropped? I know things are changing more now, what with 'Dry January' and 'Sober October', and all the non-alcoholic beers and gin and shit like that, but it's still more common to be drinking than teetotal (at least among my peers). If you go out with your mates, you basically have to justify it if you don't want to drink. People will look at you and be like, 'What the fuck's wrong with ya?' Drinking is the default. That makes it hard to resist, and so hard to quit.

I want to make it clear that I could go weeks without having a beer – I just choose not to. But I can also see how easy it would be to get stuck in that routine and spiral into a severe addiction. I think there's an assumption that men are more likely to be alcoholics than women – if you pictured an old drunk, you'd probably picture a man, right? I think that's quite a big stereotype – I know women with alcohol dependencies, who can maybe mask it a bit better. That said, the stats tell us that men are more likely to be diagnosed with alcohol disorders and are more likely to die from alcohol-related causes. The question is, why? I can imagine it's partly because men are more likely to self-medicate to numb their feelings rather than communicating and addressing them. It's easier to drown out the pain than face it. Part of that comes back to what I said in Chapter 5 – recognising that, as a man, it's okay to just be sad or angry, and talk to someone, instead of reaching for the bottle. It's okay to be vulnerable, to feel things and admit you need help.

This is all easy for me to say to you, my friend (I consider us friends now), but much harder to apply the same logic to myself. That's always the way, ain't it? It's easier to tell the people we love to look after themselves and get their act together. I remember my mum always smoked when I was growing up, and I fucking hated it and would call them 'cancer sticks'. I wanted her to look after herself and it scared me that she wasn't. And then, when she quit smoking, when I was twenty-five, I decided to take it up myself – and I've been smoking fags ever since. I don't want anyone I love to hurt themselves, but I'm happy to take the chance. It's that old hypocrisy again. Often, we know our coping mechanisms are unhealthy, but that's part of why we like them. We're punishing ourselves, because we think that's what we deserve. Maybe, in a way, we get a bit of a kick out of self-destructing. Wow, that sounds fucked up, but it's true. But I do believe, as a starting point, you have to recognise you have a problem yourself.

Drinking is a really obvious unhealthy coping mechanism, which is why I started there. But there's another one I do that can so easily slip under the radar . . . and that's keeping myself extremely busy. Some people do the opposite in hard times

– they bury their heads in the sand and avoid everything. Me? I stick my head up in the clouds. The busier you are, the harder you work and the more you focus all your energy on other people, the less time you have to sit and reflect on your own life. So I fill my time with TV jobs, podcast recordings, business ventures, meetings, social events and dates. I take on things I probably don't need to take on, like writing *Staying Relevant*'s tour, from scratch, myself. I thrive off being tired and get energy from being challenged.

I don't think that's necessarily a bad thing, but it does mean that I struggle to rest or just stop for a moment. I've mentioned before that I rarely take a holiday, and it's partly because I fill my schedule so much that I literally don't have the time. But it's also that I don't really know what to do with myself when I'm on holiday, especially the lie-by-the-pool type. I like having a purpose and, when all of that is stripped away, I feel weird and restless.

On a day-to-day basis, sleep is almost impossible for me. I'm an insomniac; I rarely sleep more than a handful of hours each night. When I tell people this, they often ask, 'What's keeping you up? What's on your mind?' They think that, if you can't slow down, it's because your thoughts are running at a million miles per hour. Don't get me wrong, I have that sometimes, but other times I'm completely blank. Sometimes I cannot rest, and I can't even pinpoint why. It's just that I don't feel right, for whatever reason. Maybe I find it hard to rest because, deep down, it makes me feel useless. If I'm not doing something productive, then what is the point in me?

It sounds like a massive contradiction to say 'resting is hard' – surely it should be the easiest thing in the world. The idea is literally that you do nothing. But I don't think I'm the only one who suffers from this inability to slow down. Maybe you're known as a workaholic or maybe you get 'productivity guilt' where you just can't sit still because you always feel like there's something else you should be doing. We're all made to believe that we're only useful if we're constantly breaking our fucking backs. Our culture was essentially built around the idea of hard graft. But actually, if you don't stop every once in a while, you'll end up making yourself sick and then you're no fucking use to anyone. Resting ain't selfish. We all need to do it. You can't fill anyone else's cup if yours is empty. I know all that, and yet it's hard to break out of the coping mechanism when it's been that way for so long. It's easier to stick to the patterns we're used to.

Then again, I stand by the fact that life would be boring if we had no discomfort and it was too peaceful and tranquil the whole time. I think everyone has this idea that they want an easy life, but do they really? We need challenges because they make us feel alive. As much as we all complain non-stop about how 'stressed' we feel, that stress normally happens because we're doing something hard and something we're passionate about. It's actually really exciting. That's why I rarely complain about how busy I am, unlike some people (yes, that's a direct dig at you, even though I don't know you . . . I'm just assuming that's what you do because every fucker does). Being busy is a privilege not everyone gets to have. As Billie Jean King said, 'pressure is a privilege'. It means you have a full life of opportunity. You, too, can choose to see it that way – it's all about shifting your perspective.

Which brings me to my next coping mechanism . . . danger. I'm a massive thrill seeker and have tried it all: every kind of rollercoaster, skydiving, cliff-diving, trying to survive on a fucking desert island and being bitten by a baby shark. If I was walking down the street and someone said, 'Do you want to jump off this building in a bungee?' I'd be like, 'Fuck it, why not?' You can't go through life wrapping yourself up in cotton wool. The way I see it, you could get hit by a car just walking on the pavement. The feeling you get after doing something that makes you scared is second to none. We all feel fear, but the more you push through it, the more you realise that fear is just something your mind has conjured up to second-guess the future. It's your brain inventing stories of what may or may not happen. You fear what you don't know. Now, I run towards that feeling because I know there's the biggest rush on the other side. Adrenaline is probably a bit like taking drugs. It's one hell of a high, and it makes me feel alive. The downside is that I actively run away from calmness and tranquillity. Danger and struggle feel more comfortable.

Lots of people are the opposite to me. Staying safe inside your comfort zone and never doing anything remotely risky is also a coping mechanism. Choosing the path of least resistance is a coping mechanism. I reckon they can both be problematic in their own ways. In the end, we use these coping mechanisms to get us through the days, but they actually just stop us living life to the full. For me, it means being unable to just slow down and feel a sense of contentment. Maybe, for you, it means you're stopping yourself from going after your dreams and ambitions because you're too afraid of what you have to lose (maybe that gets worse as we get older or after previous struggles). We need to find some balance in life, where we embrace a bit of chaos and difficulty, but we also take the time to rest and allow ourselves to feel peace – using healthy-ish means of coping and escape. Balance is the hardest fucking thing to achieve, and I'm not saying I have the answers. But acknowledging where your scales are tipping and having a bit of self-awareness for your blind spots is a good place to start.

I still think regularly about what my nan said to me that day we got our tattoos together: 'You find comfort in pain. You need to start finding comfort in happiness.' We all have our comfort zones, even if mine might look different to yours. We find comfort in our patterns and our habits, even if we know, logically, that we need to break out of them. The temptation to do what we've always done is too strong. Basically, we become addicted to our routines.

When we think about addiction, we tend to think about drinking and drugs, but you can be addicted to anything that gives you a rush. Generally, addiction starts with something that makes you feel good. But the problem with addiction is that, eventually, those good feelings stop and whatever you're doing just becomes part of your reality. The more you do something, the quicker the buzz dampens, and then it's not enough to distract you. It's never enough. It means you take it further; it becomes more extreme, because you're just chasing the high you once had. And that's when it gets dangerous and can spiral out of control.

You won't get a handle on any sort of addiction – whether it's booze, shopping, food, gambling, beauty treatments, social media, a person – unless you recognise that's what it is. What are you dependent on to get through the day? It ain't easy to admit, because there's so much stigma attached to the idea of being an 'addict'. But you're not going to be able to deal with your shit if you deny that shit exists in the first place. You know what they say: denial is just a river in Egypt. Until you recognise there's an issue or problem, you can't solve it.

First of all, don't use this recognition to beat yourself up. We all have bad habits that we should probably sack off. Yes, even that 'perfect' influencer you compare yourself to online. Trust me, the people you idolise are even more likely to be hiding their own coping mechanisms. So please remember that you're fucking normal. It's hard living in this world, and we all have to do what we can to survive. Also remember that sometimes you'll lean on your coping mechanisms more than other times. It doesn't mean you're going to be like that forever. In the past, I've felt a lot of shame for my drinking and my anger (yep, that counts as a coping mechanism too), but it's pointless to feel shame about the way you do things and then not try to change them. Shame actually keeps you stuck. It stops you from moving forward. You're human. You're going to fuck up. It's okay. Living in the past ain't gonna get you anywhere. I have learned that the hard way, but it has been useful.

It might feel impossible to imagine your life without relying on your coping mechanisms. I know I can't imagine becoming teetotal, for example. But I'm not here to advocate necessarily going cold turkey on anything. Of course, some people will need to do that. If you've hit rock bottom or you've tried everything and still can't get a handle on your addiction, then total sobriety should be the goal. Ask for help. Go to that AA or NA meeting, and do whatever else you need to get your life back and take that first step if you or those around you think it is serious. That's a medical mental health issue that I'm obviously not qualified to advise on. All I can say is: do what you have to do. It's fucking tough, because I've seen people go through it, but there'll be a lot of happiness waiting for you on the other side.

For most people and situations, I don't think it needs to be so all-or-nothing. You'll often hear celebrities or influencers or even mates saying that quitting their bad habit is the best thing they ever did. Great, that worked for them, but it might not work for you, and you don't have to be on the same path as anyone else. You can make gradual positive changes instead. The more you do something negative, the better you get at it and the more natural it becomes. The same goes for positive change. Do it more and it'll become more natural. You don't need to overhaul your whole life overnight. I know so many people who do that, but then they relapse and feel so much guilt. The tiniest changes are still changes. That might be saying, 'Actually, I'm not in the right headspace to go out today, I need to chill.' This might seem really small to you, but it's a big thing for me. I think it's called 'working on your boundaries'. If you're taking small, positive steps, you're more likely to stay on the right path, rather than falling off the fucking cliff.

Another way to get a handle on a bad habit is to start thinking about the impact it's having on the people around you. I have certainly been guilty of being self-indulgent and selfish, where I've thought, 'It's my life, and I can do what the fuck I want with it.' It's how I have justified drinking and smoking and whatever else. If I'm going to send myself into an early grave, that's my choice. It's my journey and my body, not anyone else's. Fuck everyone who judges me. Don't get me wrong, I still believe that, to an extent. But I do care about how much my coping mechanisms have an impact on the people who love and care about me. I care a lot, in fact. When my nan died, she was worried about me, and that was a fucking wake-up call. I don't want my mum or friends to have to worry about me too. If there's anything that will get you to reconsider how you behave, it's looking at your life from an outside perspective. How do your actions affect the people who love you? If you can't do it for yourself, do it for them.

One more piece of advice from your hypocritical friend (me): try something new. You never know, you might just replace your unhealthy obsessions and coping strategies with new habits that are actually beneficial. You can find things that make you feel good in a genuine way rather than, you know, a numbing, get-ready-for-the-crash kind of way. There are so many things that can give you a positive buzz – you just might not have found what it is yet. Some people find it with running, for example. It's not easy at first – in fact, it's really fucking hard – but the more you stay committed, the more you might find you enjoy it. Personally, I don't get it. I've run a few marathons in my time just to see if I could (and I could) and still never discovered that 'running high' people talk about. But different strokes for different folks – it could work for you. Or yoga. Or crafting. Again, these aren't for me, thanks, but they may be for you. Just because something saved your mate, doesn't mean it will save you. And if it doesn't, there's nothing wrong with you – it just wasn't right. Dust yourself off and try something else.

Personally, I think I need to travel more for pleasure, to get away and recharge, even though the idea of that really scares me. At the end of the day, going away is another coping mechanism. It's a way of escaping reality so that you come back more able to cope. But at least you're also enjoying new experiences and people, and looking after your mind. All of these things are coping mechanisms at the end of the day, but some are more positive than others. Try your best to swap out all the bad ones for the better ones.

That said, I'm still here at the end of this chapter doing the same bullshit I was doing at the start of it. I'm still drinking, smoking and overworking, and probably knocking years off my life in the process, but I know I am a work in progress and I am getting better. I justify it because my coping mechanisms are working. I'm coping. Still, I want life to be better than simply coping – that's just the baseline.

Living a good life is about thriving. It's about actually waking up every day and feeling excited about what's to come, rather than just being like, 'Here we go again, another day on this fucking rock.' So how do I get there? I need to take a good hard look at my life: see what's working and what isn't. Sure, all my bad habits make me feel better in the short term, but are they really helping if they're going to end up making me sick (both physically and emotionally)? Short-term solutions don't fix long-term problems. Our coping mechanisms might help us get through each day, but they won't help us get through life.

Let's break out of these patterns together. Let's stop worrying about what we regret from yesterday and start thinking about what we can do better tomorrow.

Final Fucking Thoughts: Short-term solutions don't fix long-term problems

★ We all have bad habits that help us get through the day. But are yours actually helping you cope or are they just kicking the problem down the line?

★ You won't be able to deal with your shit unless you address that the shit exists in the first place.

★ Small, positive changes can be just as effective as quitting (at least, that's what I'm telling myself).

Filming *Josh Must Win* with
Amber Gill, Vicky Pattison and
Nick Grimshaw was a right laugh

Getting my bollocks
out (for a good cause)
on *The Real Full Monty*

Talking about men's mental
health on *Loose Women*

Me, Nan and Mum

Me and my
angel of a mum

Series 11 of Celebs Go Dating in 2022

Working with Dogs Trust and U&W on a documentary to rescue, rehabilitate and rehome vulnerable dogs

Me cooking on Celebrity MasterChef

Celebrity MasterChef was an amazing experience

My kids Eric and Peggy. Not sure where I'd be without them

The world-famous bus for the *Staying Relevant* live tour!

Had to fly to Australia to support my best mate Sam on *I'm a Celeb*, didn't I?

So much love for this annoying prick, aka King of the Jungle

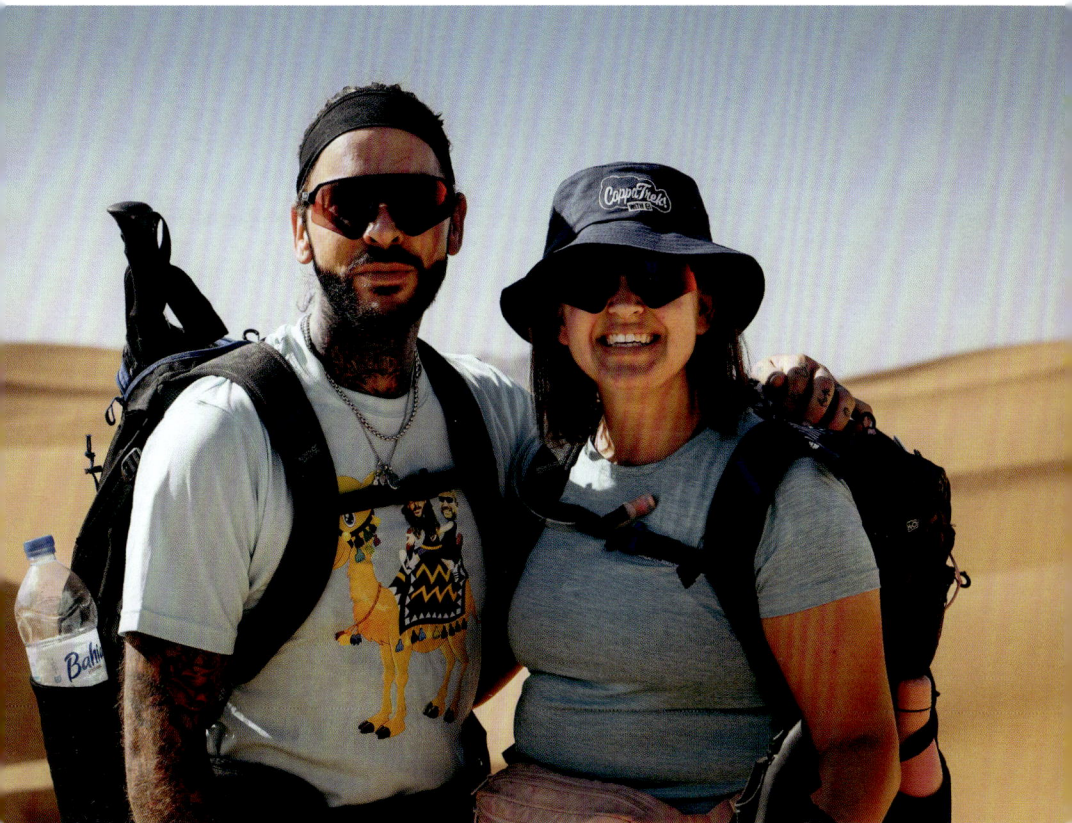

Honoured to be alongside Giovanna Fletcher, leading a group for CoppaFeel! climbing Mont Blanc

The treks I've done with CoppaFeel! have been some of the most rewarding experiences of my life

I was so up for the challenge on *Celebrity SAS: Who Dares Wins* in 2022

Gutted when I broke my ribs in the water (alongside Ashley Cain) and had to leave the show

CHAPTER 8

You Can't Do Everything,
But You Can Do Something

What gets you up in the morning? What keeps you motivated? What's your purpose in life? These are all big questions, so don't worry if you find them hard to answer. I'd struggle to answer them too. I think we all need something we're really passionate about to push us forward and keep us going every day – something that feels special and unique to us. The difficult part is working out what that shit is.

It might look like I have it all from the outside: I always have lots of bits and pieces going on, whether that's TV jobs, my podcast, charity work or whatever else. That's all fucking great, and I have loads of things that keep me motivated on a short-term basis, but I don't always know what the end-goal is. I have no fucking clue where I want to be in five years, and that scares me sometimes, given how much I like to be in control. I'm like: what am I going to be remembered for? Why am I on this planet? I'm always wondering, what's next? Big existential questions, I know.

I think these feelings are normal for everyone, but I reckon some of us are plagued with these kinds of questions more than others. Maybe you finally landed your dream role, but you can't help but think, 'Is this really what I want?' Perhaps your life feels like you're on a constant hamster wheel of work and socialising, and you'd love to do more to help your community, but don't know where to start. Many of us feel lost at different points in life, unsure of which path we should be on. It's a frustrating feeling and there is so much pressure to know what the right answer or path should be.

I'm aware that I have the most ridiculous job in the world. I actually struggle calling it 'work' because it doesn't feel like that, most of the time. The stuff you see is basically just me having fun and fucking about. The behind-the-scenes parts feel more like work, though. Again, I'm not saying I have a difficult job by any stretch of the imagination – that's just an insult to people with actually hard jobs like doctors and teachers – but, like with anything you have to do to get paid, there are bits I don't enjoy, like press interviews, endless meetings, admin and needing to be 'always on'.

Whatever way you slice it, I don't think there's such a thing as a 'dream job'. We've all been fed a lie. Working is still working at the end of the day, and we shouldn't pin all our hopes, dreams and identities on what we do for a living. I know that, for a lot of people, their job is their whole life's purpose. Whether that's helping kids or fixing drains, I think it's fucking amazing if your job makes you feel excited to wake up every morning. But, if it doesn't, it's not the end of the world. You're not a failure. No matter what you do for a living, you can still find a sense of fulfilment outside of your day job. Working should basically just give you opportunities to find your purpose – it doesn't need to be the be-all and end-all. Your talents, skills and the things you're passionate about won't necessarily be tied to how you earn money, and that's okay. Just because you're not paid to be a writer, doesn't mean you ain't a writer. Just because you're not paid to care for people, doesn't mean you don't care for people. Consider this your first 'Pete's Pep Talk' of this chapter (don't worry, there are more coming soon).

Anyway, the parts of my job that I do feel profoundly grateful for are the ones that have allowed me to have once-in-a-lifetime opportunities. I've already mentioned how much I gravitate towards activities that make me feel alive. I'm always looking for opportunities to step outside the normality of everyday life, which can be difficult because I'm also obsessed with being productive. So when I get to have these amazing experiences *and* can call them work, I feel like the luckiest fucker on the planet.

I've done some pretty incredible things since I've been a TV person, including *Celebrity MasterChef* where I got to learn about cooking from some of the best chefs in the industry. I can't have been too bad, because I made it to the quarterfinal (I will admit, I still don't cook a lot, but at least I know I can). One of my biggest highlights, though, was going on *Celebrity Island with Bear Grylls*. The idea of the show sounded really appealing to me: a bunch of random celebrities get dumped on a desert island for a month to see if they can survive on their own. I know this is most people's idea of hell, but, to me, I thought: what could be a bigger thrill? What's a bigger test than stripping back everything you have and take for granted, and throwing yourself into another world, to see if you're really the person you think you are? When all your creature comforts and support systems are taken away, who the fuck are you?

It turns out that I had a lot of the qualities I expected. I could be controlling and overbearing. Me and James Cracknell sort of took charge of the camp. I do think it's important to have people who are willing to lead in these situations. We wanted people to have food, so we took it upon ourselves to provide every single day, and we assigned jobs so that everyone played a role towards the group effort. Our intentions were good, but we didn't necessarily go about it in the right way. We became overbearing, really. I'll admit that. It was quite a big lesson that actually applies to all aspects of my life (including dating): the best intentions don't necessarily reap the best outcomes. You might think you know best for people, but often you don't, and doing 'the best' for someone actually means listening to them, rather than steamrolling over them.

That show had its hard moments, that's for sure. I'm not going to talk about the pig incident – it's a sore spot for me – but I will say that this helped me realise just how important animals are to me (which we'll come on to in a little bit). I don't necessarily regret the decisions I made, but I regret what happened and how I handled things.

The biggest lesson for me was that everyone has a safety net, even the most seemingly independent people. Even me. My nan was still alive at that time and I realised just how much I relied on her. I couldn't give a fuck about not being on social media or going out with my mates, but the one thing that weighed on me was not being able to check in on my nan and make sure she was okay. We had never gone more than a few days without speaking my whole life. I missed having her comfort and reassurance like nothing else. When all the things we take for granted are taken away from you, it changes how you view your life. It makes you realise what you can easily live without and what you really can't. It made me so much more grateful for my nan, but even more fearful about losing her.

Don't get me wrong, it was a TV show. It's entertainment, but I think I did find myself a bit on that show (as cringey as that sounds). It was a reality check in the best way possible. You know by now how much I hate feeling useless, so I loved the feeling of providing sustenance for a group of people. Waking up in the morning before dawn to catch ten fish and bring them back to the camp – that was one of the most fulfilling experiences of my life. Obviously, I know we were on telly, so the producers would never have let us die, but it did feel like I was helping people to survive another day. That made me feel good about myself. I wasn't perfect on that show, but I did my best. That applies to life too.

Same goes for when I got to go on *SAS: Who Dares Wins*. Again, not most people's idea of fun, but I wanted to unlock a different side of myself. I like to be in control of situations, but I viewed this as a chance to relinquish control and see how the fuck I'd react. Unfortunately, my first experience was cut short thanks to injuring myself, but my second time was a real test. In some ways, I passed; in others, I failed. Whatever way you look at it, the second time was extremely confronting. And I probably wouldn't be writing this book had it not been for that experience. Sometimes the hardest moments in your life are also the most necessary for growth.

There's a lot of work I do which is great experience but isn't always as glamourous in reality, but then there are the jobs I live for – the ones where I get to test my limits. I want to do things where I have no idea how good I'll be. I want to find out whether I am enough or whether I'm not. Maybe that comes from a deep-seated feeling of assuming I'm not enough. I'm looking for ways to prove this idea wrong. Maybe pushing myself in these work situations feels like a safe space to try to overcome my insecurities. They are a way for me to keep asking the question, 'Am I enough?' And, despite all these incredible experiences, I'm still not sure I've found the answer.

Wow, that got deep real quick, didn't it? Let's move swiftly on, shall we?

I do admit that working in the entertainment industry isn't completely devoid of purpose. It's a great way to connect with people. It's amazing that acting like a twat on camera can make someone feel happy – and I love making people happy, so that part is extremely rewarding.

To be honest, I never wanted to start *Staying Relevant*, the podcast I share with my best mate Sam. Sam forced me (as he always does) and basically tricked me into showing up at the studio for the first time. Like most things I assume will be utter shit, it turned out to be one of the best things we could've done.

Not just because I get to hang out with my best mate every Friday, but because it has now become even bigger than we could've imagined.

The kinds of messages we receive on a daily basis are just mind-blowing. People say they really look forward to it, and it has become a part of their life (every Monday, Thursday, Friday, SUNDAY! If you know, you know). We've had some really special messages too. There was one woman who told us she had suffered a miscarriage and listening to our podcast was the first time she had laughed in weeks. I don't take that lightly. I know that we're in a really privileged position to be able to make someone's day. I'm sure we ruin a lot of people's days too, but they can go fuck themselves.

We genuinely didn't expect the podcast to be as successful as it has been, and we definitely didn't expect our tour to sell out as quickly as it did. Having so many people queue up for tickets, be so excited when they got them and come out to see two idiots prance around on stage for a couple of hours was wild and humbling.

When it came to doing the tour, we were offered writers to help us come up with it, but, me being me, I wanted to test myself. So I thought, 'Fuck it – I'll give it a go.' I knew that taking on the entire show was a lot of pressure and I could fall flat on my ass, but I live for the challenge. And the gamble seemed to pay off – the feedback we received was fucking unbelievable. We had to put on a few extra dates just to deal with the demand.

To make up for the egotistical nonsense of my job and the fact I feel incredibly fortunate (and unworthy) for the life I lead, charity work is a big priority for me. I'm in a privileged position to have the time, resources and platform to help others and raise awareness about issues, so I try to use that opportunity to the best of my ability. I grew up watching my nan do fucking anything for anyone she met. She helped so many people over the years – whether that was letting someone sleep on her sofa or giving them advice in times of hardship. You can help people in the smallest ways, and I think I've always carried that with me. You can just give what you've got. Even before I started making a few bob, I tried my best to help people in need – that might have just meant giving £1 to a homeless person. It's all relative. I think it's all about offering what you have to give. It's no more or less than anyone else.

I find it incredible that so many people with platforms do absolutely nothing that can help in any positive or substantial way. That said, I'm not suggesting people should speak up on issues they know fuck-all about. I would never advise that – I actually think that can cause more harm than good, but you should add value with your voice when you feel you can. Of course, there's a big problem in society at the moment that says if you don't speak up on an issue, then you don't care. That's not the case – we shouldn't expect people to speak on issues when they don't know enough and don't feel comfortable. It doesn't mean they aren't moved or heartbroken by a certain cause. It's just that they're not qualified to speak on it. Also, you can't be across everything. The world is full of horrifying shit and, if we thought about every story of death, pain and destruction every minute of the day, we'd never get anything done. I think it's more than okay to choose a couple of issues that are really close to your heart (mine are dogs and animal welfare) and do everything in your power to make a difference in those specific areas. It's better to put your whole heart into one or two things than to spread your heart too thin on multiple causes and end up achieving fuck-all.

It comes back to the old social media problem again: we're bombarded with distressing images, but we have no idea what we can actually do about them. And we're expected to act or behave in a certain way, which means that people end up speaking up on issues they don't actually care or know about. They just do it because they feel pressured by their followers and want to show that they're a 'good' person. Same goes for people who post about giving money to charities, hunting for likes. It undoes the good deed if you're only doing it so that people praise you for it. I'm not saying you shouldn't raise awareness about issues – I know I've used my platform for this purpose, like doing a photo shoot for Humane Society International, the animal cruelty charity, where I was made to look like a dead animal (sexy). But I just think you should do it for the right reasons; because it's a cause close to your heart and you want to get the message out in order to make a difference. Anything you do for clicks and likes is inauthentic. I do lots of stuff behind the scenes that I wouldn't ever talk about, because I just want to help. I'm not doing it for validation.

Although, if I'm really honest with myself, I try to give as much money and time as I can, as a form of redemption for all the shit times in life. Doing good makes me feel better because it feels like I'm balancing out all the times I think I was a bad bloke. I feel guilty and privileged, so charity work helps suppress some of those feelings. So is it selfish in its own way? Maybe. Still, I think that the more you have to give, the more you *should* give. We aren't alone on this planet, we're surrounded by other people and animals and nature – and we all have a role to play in making the world a better place. You can't do everything, but you can always do something.

One of my favourite events of the year is the trek I do with breast cancer charity, CoppaFeel!. This is where the charity gathers together and helps fundraise for a group of women who have been affected by cancer in some way (whether they're going through it or they've lost someone) by taking on a huge challenge. I was brought on as a team leader, to help a group through their journey. So far, we've done treks in the Sahara Desert and the Tour du Mont Blanc – and there's hopefully another in the works that I'm gearing up for at the time of writing this. This first came about when I was hosting a different podcast years ago, and I interviewed CoppaFeel!'s amazing founder Kristin Hallenga, who has very sadly now passed away. She asked if I'd like to be involved with what they do and I said I'd love to, but I was hesitant because I wasn't sure what I'd be able to offer. It's very female-led and I thought, why would anyone want me there? How would I be able to support these women, physically and emotionally, through a challenge like this? I thought that maybe my presence would be a bit of a gimmick.

I didn't anticipate that I'd learn far more from these women than they would ever learn from me. Each year I've done it, I've led a group of thirty to forty of the most incredible women I've ever met. We start off the week as strangers and we finish as a family. It's such a special bonding experience, because you spend a week with these people, nurturing, supporting and caring for each other. I thought I would be the odd man out and they'd think I was just some tattooed idiot from reality TV, but they accepted me for who I am and made me feel like a valued member of that family. Those treks have been some of the only times in my life when I've felt genuinely at peace and content. It's wild, when you think about it, because we experienced some tough conditions, including walking for hours each day in some of the harshest terrains. I always felt like I had absolutely no excuse to crumble in front of these inspirational women, so I'd take it upon myself to carry everyone's things when they got tired. I became known as the donkey because I was always carrying something for someone.

I never minded though, because the strength and resilience of these women kept me going. The fact they could all support each other and keep pushing forward to this end-goal, through something as tragic and horrendous as cancer, was life changing. Every time I go, it reminds me to stop being such a miserable sod. I haven't quite achieved that, as you can probably tell, but we're getting there.

I'll always treasure one particular memory, on the penultimate day of the Sahara trek. We'd had a really tough day of walking; everyone's feet were in bits. We had to climb a steep mountain followed by a sand dune – it was really tough shit, particularly for some of these women who had already put their bodies through a lot to get there. When we reached the top, everyone was in tears at what they had achieved. Knowing what so many of these women had been through due to cancer – the loss of self-esteem, confidence or loved ones – and watching their belief in themselves be reignited, in real time, was extremely precious. After walking for about ten hours straight, we descended down the mountain – and we noticed a jeep that had stopped at the bottom. Bear in mind, this is the middle of the desert – we hadn't seen anyone else for miles and miles. As we got closer, we saw it was these Moroccan men in the jeep, wearing full traditional clothing. They had probably stopped to see what the fuck was going on with all these women and a hairy wally coming down the mountain.

When we reached the bottom, they started cheering and singing for us. They got out of their car and played some traditional music from the speakers, and we were all dancing, crying and cheering together. It was possibly one of the most beautiful moments of my life. It was one of those times when I had to take a step back and look at the moment from above. I just thought, 'Fuck, I'm so lucky to be here.'

There was another moment on the Mont Blanc trail that will stick with me forever. On the last day, they all made me sit down in the middle of a circle. I was like, 'What the fuck's going on here?' They had each prepared a little speech that started with, 'Pete, you're the type of man that . . .' It was painful for me, listening to people speak so nicely about me and so earnestly – I'm used to people taking the piss out of me, and me doing the exact same in return. At the same time, it was a beautiful and special experience. The fact that they'd all gone through so much and still saw a light in me was really emotional. It reminded me of my nan.

When it comes to giving back, a lot of my focus has been on animals. I'm known for my love of dogs, but all animals are important to me and I've worked closely with charities that focus on animal cruelty, and specifically the fur trade. People often ask me why I give so much of a shit about animals, when there are so many people suffering in the world as well. Of course, I know that, but, for me, it's about giving a voice to the voice-less. Animals can't advocate for themselves, so they need us to do it for them.

I feel more at home around animals than people anyway. We always had cats growing up, and my first dog was a rescue dog called Arnie. He ended up at a shelter because he'd been dumped by his owners by the side of the road. He walked miles back to the house where he lived, but his former owners had moved, so the new owners took him into the shelter. They called him Arnie, short for Arnold Schwarzenegger – based on his famous Terminator quote, 'I'll be back.' I loved that dog with everything I had, and every animal that came after. I think I've always had an affinity to animals – especially dogs – because they live for the moment. They don't care what you look like, what you've been through or where you're going. They don't ask questions. They just want to love you and be loved in return. They're so simple, yet so complex. They feel your pain and know what to do when you're in pain. They calm, they soothe and they have no bad intentions. I feel so happy and peaceful just being in their presence.

I've been to fur farms and dog meat farms, and I've seen how badly dogs and other animals have been hurt and mistreated, and it just reminds me how fucking disgusting humans are. It makes me feel so ashamed. And yet, when you show an ounce of compassion and empathy towards an animal, they give it right back. I went to South Korea with Humane Society International not too long ago to find out more about the dog meat trade (which is, thankfully, now illegal thanks to our campaigning). We went to one farm and rescued 174 dogs to be rehomed in America and the UK. It was on this farm that I met a Japanese Tosa called Angel. Japanese Tosas are one of those 'bad breeds' that are considered dangerous, and are therefore used as status symbols for fucking dickheads. In my opinion, no dog is born bad – they just have characteristics that make them more dangerous and can be trained to become more aggressive (usually using fear tactics – dogs generally attack when they're afraid).

Anyway, Angel was a huge dog and she was kept in her own cage in a different part of the farm because she was so reactive; she was always growling and aggressive. I could tell as soon as I looked at her that she was petrified of the world. This came out as aggression, but it was pure fear. Her interactions with humans had never been good – she had been mistreated and abused. But I quietly sat by the side of her cage and, eventually, she started to calm down and slowly came towards me. After about twenty minutes of silence, she understood that I wasn't going to harm her and she allowed me to gently touch her head without growling. Two hours later, I was in the cage with her. She wasn't a bad dog. She'd just had horrendously bad experiences.

My Peggy is the same. I rescued her from being put down after she had bitten another dog. I just socialise her slowly and tune into what she needs. Humans often think they can force dogs into behaving a certain way, but they're dogs at the end of the day. They don't just exist to serve us and our needs. Not all dogs are perfect – and, yes, some of them are nuts – but, just like with most humans, I strongly believe that some dogs can be rehabilitated after previous trauma. This is of course a separate conversation to the seriousness of dangerous dogs. Like with anything, there's a clear line between rehab and animals behaving dangerously towards humans and children.

I've always loved dogs and it's been so rewarding rehoming and working with charities like Dogs Trust. Sometimes, again, like humans they can be misunderstood – they crave unconditional love but their fear can take over, especially when they've come from a previous home where they haven't been treated well.

My work and my charity projects give me a sense of purpose; they give me goals that I can work towards. It's great, but I know that, once I achieve one, I find myself another one. And then another one. And then another one. The cycle continues on and on, and yet I still don't know what the big overarching goal for my life is. I don't think I'm any closer to answering those questions: why am I here? What's my purpose in life?

Sometimes it's nice to take a step away from these existential

questions and just be in the moment. I know I can be so preoccupied with worrying about the future and overthinking shit
that I forget to be present and just live for now. The main way I
do that is by getting on my motorbike. It is my ultimate means
of escape.

I've always had a fascination with bikes, as my dad was into
them too. My mum hated the idea of me ever getting on a bike
because they're known to be dangerous. So, of course, one of
the first things I did when I moved out was go, 'I can do what I
fucking want,' and I bought my first bike. I don't just love it
because it's rebellious. I mean, yeah, there's something cool
about being a biker – no denying that. But I love the sense of
peace it gives me. When I get on my bike, I'm not thinking of
anything else. It's like a blank space – the perfect way to clear
my head. I can't meditate because I can't sit still for shit, but
biking is like my form of meditation. That might sound weird to
you, but people do all sorts of weird shit to calm themselves
down and this is just mine.

When I decide I'm having a bike day, I turn off my phone
when I'm riding – which means three to five hours at a time
without my phone on. I don't think about anything, but I might
listen to some fucking good music to unwind. It's weird because
riding bikes is a very independent, solo thing, but I also ride with
other people – and it's such a lovely community. I've made
some great mates; we've bonded over our love for Harley-
Davidsons. It's nice to be in a community where you share a
common interest and no one really cares who you are or what
you do for a living. I don't really have that in other parts of my

life. When I go out, I'm often approached by people who recognise me or ask for pictures. Don't get me wrong, it's lovely that people want to stop and chat. But, sometimes, when I am not having the best day, it's a reminder of my work and it keeps me in a state of 'always on'. When I'm out with the biking community, they'll just say things like, 'I like the seat on your bike,' or 'That's a lovely exhaust.' And I'll go, 'Thanks, it's new, I just had it fitted.' Probably fucking uninteresting to most people, but we love it – and there's something special about that.

I try to go on a couple of biking trips every year. I've toured places like Hungary, Italy, Ireland and Scotland – and these are like my small breaks from reality. As I've said, I don't tend to take proper holidays, but these trips are my way of escaping, whenever I can. There's something about whizzing through country roads, feeling free with the wind in your hair, that is so refreshing. It makes me feel like I'm really living. I'm pretty sure every biker says that, and non-bikers wouldn't understand it. But I think we can all find that 'thing' that makes us feel this way.

We all need a release from the mundane shit that we do. Yes, even me, whose job is generally good fun. It doesn't matter what your job is – you could have the best job in the world, but you'll still find that you're constantly doing the same shit and there will be elements you want to escape from. It's nice having something that gets you away from your work life. I think there's this idea that you have to turn your hobbies into a career. I think that's bullshit. If anything, it's good to keep your hobby sacred. Turning it into work can suck the joy out of it.

Whatever your 'thing' is, I think there's something particularly precious about having a hobby that gets you out into nature. I'm not saying you need to go hug a tree or climb a mountain, but spending time in the great outdoors gives you perspective. We move through the world thinking we, and our problems, are so fucking important. Sometimes it takes looking out at a beautiful view of the ocean or looking up at the stars in the sky to think: 'Hang on, none of that shit is important. I'm just a tiny speck on this planet, and so are my silly little issues.' I know that's quite a hippie way of looking at it, but we all need reminders sometimes about how big the world is. I'm a city boy in my bones, but being in the city can sometimes feel like you're wading through shit – both physically and metaphorically. Stepping away from the everyday humdrum of life is healing.

The important thing is to find something that doesn't have an end-goal. So much of life is about taking stepping stones – you're saving for a house, or aiming for a job, or working towards having kids. You're always moving in a certain direction. Ironically, physically moving on my bike is actually an opportunity to stand still. When we ride, we don't always have a specific end location in mind. The goal is simply to enjoy the journey. A lot of people don't really understand that. In fact, Sam will sometimes say to me: 'What, you mean you just ride around for a few hours without going anywhere?' But that's the point. There isn't a target. There's no goal. The only goal is to make memories, and just be. We all need something like this in life, because, when we're constantly striving towards goals, we never feel content. It's never enough. There's always another target to be hit.

I'd say that bikes are my form of 'self-care', but that word makes me cringe a bit. I know it shouldn't, but I think it's that old toxic masculinity thing again. It seems almost weak to say: 'I need some fucking time out to recharge.' I know that so many people feel this sense of guilt, because we're all so busy and have so many responsibilities and people who rely on us. But, speaking from a male perspective, I've noticed that men can be particularly resistant to the whole idea of 'self-care'. They feel like they need to have a reason to take a step back. I'm definitely guilty of that, which means often I don't take those bike days unless I really, really need them. I get to a point where I'm completely burned out, so going on the bike is almost like a last-ditch attempt to get some sanity back. It shouldn't be like that. We should treat mental health preventatively, rather than reacting to low periods when we have them. I shouldn't need a reason to press pause. The reason is just that I'm looking after myself, so that I can come back to all my responsibilities feeling fresher and more motivated. I tend to live a life of incredible highs and crashing lows. But it would probably be more sustainable and cleverer if I worked on preventing the dips and keep getting on my bike, even when I don't think I need it.

Writing all this stuff has actually made me realise a few things. First, maybe I'm not as lost as I thought I was. I actually do have things I am passionate about: I have work, causes and hobbies that keep me motivated. Maybe it just doesn't always feel that way because I think there should be one common thread that unites all the different parts of me. But actually, does there need to be? I'm starting to think maybe it's okay for my purpose to keep moving and changing. Maybe it's alright that I have no idea where the fuck I'll be in five years. In fact, that might even be a good thing. We don't know what the future holds, so what's the fucking point in trying to control it all the time?

Don't get me wrong, I think it's great to have goals and dreams. But I think we have to be open to them changing. Back in the day, my goal was to run my own recruitment company. That fell by the wayside, but it got replaced with lots of fucking amazing opportunities. And who knows, I could still end up doing it one day. If you have a dream, that's great. But I'd say, don't be so fixated on it that you don't notice other opportunities that come your way. Don't be afraid to change your dream halfway through. There's no goal police making sure you're staying on track. It might seem weird to other people – like if you quit your job as a lawyer to become a scuba-diving instructor. But it doesn't need to make sense to anyone else; it only has to make sense to you.

Similarly, if you're none the wiser about what your purpose or dream is, that's okay too. There's this idea that if you're not sure where you want to be in the future and you're not working towards something, you're lazy or not ambitious. Obviously, that can be true sometimes. But, a lot of the time, you just haven't found the thing that will get you up in the morning and make you feel excited. There's no need to force it, even if everyone around you is telling you that you need to have life figured out. Tell them to 'fuck off'. It's your life – not anyone else's. You can take as much time as you need. Also, you do not have to love your job. It doesn't have to be your sole purpose. It's okay to just work to earn money and spend the rest of your life finding other things to live for – whether that's volunteering, travelling the globe, making music or whatever. Just because you ain't making money from it, doesn't mean it's not important. There are so many ways you can contribute to the world with your skills and gifts that are completely separate to what you do for work.

If you're feeling especially lost in life, I recommend volunteering as a great way to find a sense of motivation again. Not only is it rewarding to help people (or animals, or the planet), it's also a great way to find a sense of community. The people I met on my CoppaFeel! treks changed my life and my whole perspective. You can find these life-changing people, and life-changing moments, if you look for them. This shit is possible for every single one of you. If you feel passionate about a specific cause, reach out to a charity and ask what they need, or pop into one of their centres or shops to see how you can get involved. Most charities are desperate for people who want to help, and you can usually use your specific skills and talents and work it around your life and schedule. Trust me, it always feels good when you feel like you're making a difference – even in the smallest ways.

Maybe you're reading this and you're feeling motivated to take your career into a new direction. Like with friendships and dating, it again comes back to being proactive. You can't wait for opportunities to land in your lap; you have to go out looking for them. Email people at companies you want to work for and ask if they're free for a coffee. Introduce yourself. Granted, 99 per cent of them will probably ignore you and/or tell you to 'fuck off'. But that 1 per cent could change your life – you just won't know unless you try. And it's more than likely that you won't achieve the thing you want straight away. Sometimes you put a shit-ton of work in and it doesn't reap the results you want. That's part of life. But just remember that everything you're doing is a lesson learned. It's easy to think, 'What was the point in all that?' when you don't see an instant result. Remember that the result is coming, in one way or another; you just don't know what it is yet. All the setbacks are nudging you towards something good.

Maybe *you're* not as lost as you think you are, either. You're just finding your way. You don't need to have a clear purpose. You don't need an obvious end-goal. Your purpose can change by the day. Maybe, today, it's just helping an old dear cross the road. Maybe you've had very down days in the past where getting out of bed and having a shower is your only purpose. And maybe, in future, your purpose will be performing in front of a crowd of 6,000 people. Goals can be big and small. They're all important, but also not fucking important at all. Does that make sense?

I guess what I'm trying to say is: don't get so hung up on the future. Don't worry about where your career is going or whether you're doing enough for the world to make a difference. Do what you can, every day, and don't be afraid to re-evaluate and take a step back. And make sure you find moments to switch off from all that shit, to just exist. Float in the ocean. Lie on the grass and listen to music. You don't always have to be useful . . . says the man who hates feeling useless. I'm going to take my own advice though, so I'm going for a ride on my motorbike before we get into the next chapter. Buckle up, it's going to be a sad one.

Final Fucking Thoughts: You can't do everything, but you can do something

- ★ It's better to put your heart into one or two causes that you really care about than to spread yourself too thin and end up achieving fuck-all.
- ★ You don't need to have one life's purpose; your purpose can change every day. On one day, having a shower might be your biggest achievement – that's okay.
- ★ We all need some kind of hobby that we do just for the sake of it, without any goal in mind. We all need a release from the mundane shit we do, and the constant question: 'what next?'

CHAPTER 9

You've Got Through the Worst Shit Before. You Can Do It Again

I've got to be real with you for a second: I haven't been completely honest. Well, I haven't *lied*, but I've been holding back. There was something that happened when I was a kid that contributed to a lot of the issues I've outlined in this book – the anger, the feelings of uselessness, the need to be independent, the fear of never being enough. It's difficult for me to talk about, because it's not just my story – it's also my mum's. But I think I need to grow some fucking balls and address it, so that everything else makes a bit more sense. As I've been preaching the whole way through this book, you have to confront your past if you want to build a better future.

Before I get into it, I want to make it very clear that my mum is my hero. She's the most loving, giving, beautiful person I've ever known. She's not massively loud and outgoing like I am, but she's so empathetic, forgiving and sensitive. Despite all the shit I've put her through, she has always seen the best in me. She did her best to hide the harder parts of life from me for most of my childhood. She protected me, shielded me from her heartbreaks, and gave me the best upbringing she possibly could.

When Nan was alive, the three of us described ourselves as the Three Musketeers. Nan was 'the person' for both of us, and now we're trying to be that for each other. Mum'd do fucking anything for me and I'm the same with her. I don't blame her for any of the shit that happened. At least, not anymore. I know better now.

I was twelve years old at the time. I've already told you about my parents' divorce, which threw everything up in the air. It was a really messy time for a while. Mum was on-and-off with her new fella for a few months (he was navigating his own breakup and family dynamics) and obviously we had to move house, which made everything feel a bit unsettled. It was quite a complicated, turbulent time, so it didn't surprise me that Mum seemed sad. I didn't think she appeared any worse than I would've expected for the situation. She was great with me – always just trying to make sure I was okay and well looked after. I didn't have a fucking clue what was going on inside her head.

The first thing I noticed was that she was drinking more than usual. Mum had always loved a drink, but it was never out of hand. She was just very sociable and I often saw her drinking with her mates. I didn't know, at the time, that drinking was a coping mechanism for her. She told me this had started before I was born. Nan would later tell me that my mum had suffered from depression throughout her youth, but she had managed to keep it contained when she was raising me. Nan said that having a family seemed to stabilise her, and she was fine for a while.

The end of her marriage seemed to trigger a series of events that reignited some of Mum's demons. After many years of putting her mental health on the back-burner, everything came back up to the surface again. She started drinking more, alone at home, when previously she had only done that with friends. To this day, she views drink as a massive contributing factor to worsening her mental state. The problem is, it felt like a coping mechanism at the time – but, in the end, it did more damage than it did helping her cope.

Anyway, I have tried to replay the build-up over and over in my head, looking for signs that she desperately needed help. Even the drinking didn't seem particularly worrying. She seemed to have a handle on it. I didn't expect her to explode in the way she did. To be honest, I didn't even know people did that sort of shit.

It was a really dark, rainy night. I'm not even saying that for dramatic effect – I don't remember much, but I do remember it was really fucking horrible outside, almost like a horror movie. Tony wasn't around at that point – I'm not sure where he was. I think they were on one of their breaks while he tried to deal with his own family shit. I sat at the kitchen table with Mum while she drank wine and cried. I can't remember what exactly had happened that day or what had triggered it, but I know I was trying to comfort her, but had no idea what to do. 'Don't worry about me darling, I'm fine,' she kept saying through her sobs, 'you can go to bed, I'm fine. I just want to be on my own.' I didn't believe she was fine, but I was out of ideas for how I could help. She insisted she wanted some space and I worried I was making things worse for her by being there, so eventually I agreed to go upstairs.

I thought I'd just play a game or something, but I couldn't concentrate on anything while I could still hear her crying downstairs. I felt sick leaving her sitting there. I'm not sure how much time passed, but I could hear her cries become more and more uncontrollable, and I knew I couldn't stay upstairs any longer. So I went downstairs and, when I turned the corner into the kitchen, I saw her sitting at the table, which had become covered in blood. I saw the blood dripping first, and then I looked up to see that it was coming from Mum's wrists. She was holding a knife in her other hand.

Immediately, I ran over to her to take the knife from her hand. Before that, she had seemed almost possessed – it was like my mum had gone and someone (or something) else had taken over her body. But when I came over to her, it's like she woke up. She looked up at me with eyes full of tears. She looked so ashamed.

'I'm so sorry,' she said. 'I'm so sorry, I'm so sorry,' she kept repeating. I told her it was okay as I panicked trying to work out what to do. I called Nan. I could barely get the words out to describe what had happened. I think I basically just said, 'Mum . . . knife . . . wrists . . . blood.' But Nan knew what to do. She calmly told me to hang up and call an ambulance, and that she'd get a taxi over as soon as possible. I took her instructions, calling the ambulance, and then I got to work trying to look after Mum, who by that point was sitting on the floor and bleeding very badly. I grabbed towels and put them around her wrists to try to dress them and stop the bleeding. I poured the wine down the sink. She was drowsy, but she kept repeating the words: 'I'm sorry, I'm so sorry.'

It's hard to pinpoint how I felt in that moment, because I think it was just pure shock. I didn't cry – I just went into crisis mode. I became protective, like the only thing I could do was look after Mum and make sure she survived this. I didn't say it, but I believed it was my fault. I had been with Mum before it happened. I had agreed to go upstairs. I had stayed upstairs even though I could hear her wailing. If it was anyone's fault, it was mine.

Looking back, I know that my responsibility was probably overwhelming in that moment. I was the child, and I needed to be looked after. Instead, I had to look after my parent and suppress all the fear, panic, loneliness and self-blame that was beginning to grow inside me. I've said multiple times in this book that I grew up quickly, and I've often credited that to hanging around with older people. But I think a lot of it comes back to this moment. From that point onwards, I wasn't a kid anymore. I had to be the provider and protector. I had to be strong. I decided I would never be as useless as I was that day. Uselessness is my worst nightmare.

I can't really remember the rest of what happened that night, so I've pieced together this information over the years from a combination of my own memories, and what Nan and Mum told me. The ambulance came and took Mum off to hospital, and Nan arrived to finally be the reassuring, calming voice I needed. In the end, Mum was treated for her wounds and it turned out the damage wasn't as bad as it looked. She'd only nicked an artery and we found out she'd be absolutely fine. But it was clear she had tried to take her own life, and it would've been worse if she hadn't received help in time. She didn't want to be here anymore. She told me later that the moment I found her was a big realisation for her. Me seeing her like that made her think: 'What the fuck am I doing?' So, once she had been bandaged up, she took herself to a mental hospital and voluntarily admitted herself.

The next morning, though, I woke up and she was back home. She later told me she woke up the next morning in hospital feeling so ashamed, and just thought, 'Fuck, I shouldn't be here. People need me.' So she discharged herself and walked an hour and a half back home. Nan had stayed over, and we were both shocked to see her back. She looked absolutely dreadful and was still wearing her hospital wristband. I remember her snipping it off straight into the bin and being so apologetic. 'I'm so sorry, it was a moment of madness and it will never happen again, I promise,' she kept repeating. I didn't really want to talk about it, so I just said, 'It's fine, don't worry about it, it's all good.' I think I was worried that, if we communicated in any more detail, all the feelings I was trying to suppress would spill out of me.

One of those feelings was anger. I was angry at her for doing it. She kept telling me she loved me and she was sorry, but I thought: how could you love me, if you would've fucking left me? I thought I wasn't enough for her to stay. As well as blaming myself for leaving her there at the table, I also blamed her. Suicide (and attempted suicide) comes with so many complicated feelings of guilt and blame, which I didn't really know how to process at the time. The whole situation just made me feel awful, and I didn't know what to do with all those emotions. I guess that's where this whole problem stemmed from in the first place. Mum didn't know how to deal with all her intense emotions. She spent so long suppressing them and trying to cope, until they eventually exploded in the worst way. It just shows that nothing good comes from attempting to bottle this shit up inside.

The aftermath was a bit of a blur, as Mum tried to make everything feel normal again. But we had only just gotten the blood stains out of the floorboards. Nothing was really normal. I remember being terrified for a really long time. I hated the idea of leaving her on her own. I think she overcompensated, trying to appear cheerful, playing music and cooking nice meals. It could be unnerving.

Over time, my nerves settled. Even though Mum had discharged herself from being an inpatient, she was required to have a psychiatric assessment and they diagnosed her with bipolar disorder (they called it manic depression at the time). I didn't know what it was, but I later learned it's a mental illness where sufferers experience severe depression alongside hypomanic episodes where they might seem extremely happy. She started taking medication for it, which seemed to steady her, and she went to therapy to help her understand her triggers. She was also wise enough to know that the alcohol had been a big catalyst for what happened. Even though she'd used it all her life as a numbing agent, it ended up heightening her feelings and had a drastic outcome. She quit altogether for a long time.

Nothing came up again for several years. I didn't want to talk to Mum about it, but I'd speak to Nan about it occasionally. I would tell her about how I blamed myself, and how I blamed Mum, for what happened – and she'd just listen without judging me. She had a way of doing that. I know she really worried about Mum though. Towards the end of her life, she would say to me, 'You need to look after Tracy.' We both always had that fear that something could knock her off her feet again. I avoided speaking to Mum directly about it, because I already knew she carried a lot of guilt and shame over what happened. I know that she still does. I never wanted to tell her I was angry with her or that I felt like she'd let me down, because she didn't need it at that time. I just wanted her to focus on getting better and moving forward in life. I didn't want her to feel any worse than she did already.

It's only in the last few years that I've processed a lot of what has happened and I've had some really open conversations with her. I have come to understand that she never wanted to leave me – she wanted to leave herself. It wasn't because she didn't love me enough. It's because the struggle and the pain was so real that she wasn't able to think outside of that. Logical and rational thinking didn't come into the equation. What she had (or didn't have, or whatever else) became irrelevant in that moment. She was looking for a way to escape the pain she was in. She thought it was a moment of clarity, but actually it was the exact opposite of that. It was the complete antithesis of clarity. That moment was born out of pure pain, sadness and every negative emotion you can imagine. All of that combined into a cocktail of shite where she believed, in that moment, that what she was doing would be the only way out. I know that's not particularly eloquent, but what I'm trying to say is: you can't blame people for how they feel. The problem isn't the people who try to take their own lives. The problem is all the pain and trauma that leads them to that decision. I don't blame my mum for any of it. I just wish I could take all that pain away.

Unfortunately, things got bad again not too long ago. It was a few months after Nan died. I think me and Mum were trying our best to support each other. We had both lost our person, and I know Nan had told us each separately when she died to look after each other, so that's what we were trying to do. As a result, Mum seemed to be handling Nan's death reasonably well. But then, only a few weeks later, Mum lost her brother – my uncle, Stephen.

He had been ill for a couple of years, so it wasn't completely unexpected. I was away at the time on my trek with CoppaFeel!, but Mum didn't tell me until I landed back in the UK. I was like, 'Why didn't you fucking tell me?' She said she didn't want me to fly home (because she knew I would've). 'You were with people who needed you more than I do,' she said. She seemed quite calm, so I wasn't overly worried, but, of course, I always had the niggling voice in the back of my head: will this tip her over the edge again? And, if it does, will I be able to do something to stop it?

A few weeks later, I got a call from Tony. Him and Mum were on their way back from a party. Mum had started drinking again a few years before – only a little bit, for social occasions. She knew how badly it affected her, so she was good at sticking to only one or two glasses. This time, she had been drinking a lot, and she was very drunk. 'She keeps talking about Stephen lying on a slab,' Tony told me. 'And how all she wants is you.'

It was fucking raining again that night. I jumped on my motorbike in the pouring rain and arrived at their house before they got home. Tony opened Mum's car door and she looked like a fucking mess. She had been crying the whole way, so there was make-up running down her face. We brought her inside and sat her down. She kept talking; she was delirious and not making much sense. She just kept repeating that Stephen was lying on a slab, and how much she wished Nan was there. Then she said, 'I don't want to be here anymore.' It was the first time I had heard her say something like that since that night, almost two decades previously.

In that moment, I felt like I was twelve years old again. I saw the panic on Tony's face and I saw how distressed Mum was, and I just thought: 'No. This isn't happening again. I'm an adult now. I'm not useless. This time, I can help.' So I tried to channel Nan. I thought, what would Nan do? She'd just listen. She'd just be there, without judging. So I sat down with Mum on the sofa. I put a blanket over her and made her a coffee. And I just listened to her incoherent ramblings and told her it was all going to be okay. Eventually, she sobered up and started making a bit more sense, and I just stayed with her, talking about Nan and Stephen until the early morning. Just like that night all those years before, she apologised profusely. I told her she didn't need to say sorry. She was allowed to hurt. I mean, fuck me, the world is brutal, ain't it? She'd just lost her mum and brother – she had every right to be upset. I was just glad she allowed me to help her, and sit with her, this time.

When she started drifting off, I put her to bed. She was a lot calmer, and Tony told me to go home and he'd call me in the morning. I thought I was fine, but then I rode my bike home and, as soon as I got through the front door, I broke down. I was never going to let her see how much her state affected me while I was there, because I deal with my shit on my own. I always have. It's not the right way, but it's my way, and, as you know, I'm working on that.

Instead of getting angry – my usual habit before Nan died – I just balled my fucking eyes out like a little baby. But then it helped me see things more clearly. I felt reassured that this time was different to last time. I know she said she didn't want to be here anymore, but I knew she didn't mean it. This time, it was more of a cry for help, rather than a genuine urge to end her life. I also felt glad that, this time, she had asked for me. I'm pleased she allowed me to be there for her. Nan had told me to look after Mum – and, thankfully, this time I was able to. I couldn't before. I was too young to know what was going on or how to behave. But this time I could.

The next day, I called Mum and she apologised again and again. She admitted that she shouldn't have had anything to drink that night. She was feeling too vulnerable, and the drink tipped her into an unhealthy headspace. I knew it wouldn't ever be like how it was before, but it did go to show that however long it has been, or however much of a handle you think you have on your demons, you carry so much with you. I think everything accumulated that night: all the pain she had suppressed from losing Nan and then her brother. It's a reminder that shit doesn't go away. It can always be dredged up again. It isn't enough to just say, 'I'm good now. I'm okay now.' You have to keep working on it every day and live alongside it. You have to make a conscious effort to keep having more good days than bad.

That's exactly what Mum has always done. It was a moment of difficulty, but I'm so fucking proud of all the work she has done on herself over the years to avoid being in that place. She's the strongest person I know. To go all the way to rock bottom, and to come back with even more empathy and love than before? It's nothing short of amazing. I admire anyone who is able to do that. Thanks to a lot of therapy and self-reflection, I know Mum has come to a place where she has accepted herself and doesn't feel as much guilt as she used to. She knows that she hasn't always been herself when the depression has taken over, but she forgives herself and knows that she still has purpose and worth. She knows how much she means to people – or at least, I hope she does.

I think we could all do with learning that from my mum. You can say to yourself: 'I'm a lovely person, even if I have made mistakes or fucked up in the past.' I've said it before, but I'll say it again: self-love isn't about saying, 'I'm the best person on this planet.' It's about finding that comfortable, rational middle ground in between 'I'm the most amazing person ever,' and 'I'm fucking horrendous.' Something I've noticed is that the people who are most compassionate to others are often the least compassionate to themselves. Mum is definitely like this. I think she has given so much of her love and energy to other people that she doesn't have any left to pour into herself. I'm not saying I'm the most compassionate bloke on the planet, and I'm nowhere near the kind of person my mum is, but I think I'm guilty of doing this too. I find it so much easier to be compassionate to other people than I do to myself. My dial tends to spin towards 'I'm the worst person in the world,' but I'm doing my best to push it the other way. It's okay to have bad feelings about yourself every once in a while, but you just want enough good feelings that you can override the shit ones.

I like to think all of my best qualities come from my mum. But I also think there's some fragility I share with her as well. The insecurity, the self-doubt, internalising emotions because she wants to be strong for everyone else . . . I relate to all of these things. But seeing her hit rock bottom motivated me in some ways, because I don't ever want to end up there. I don't want her (or anyone else) to have to see me in that state, because I have seen the ripple effects. I'm not going to lie, I love the idea of having kids in the future, but I'm scared of it too. I found out recently that mental ill health runs in my family. Mum's brother had schizophrenia. Her dad suffered from depression, and his mum (Mum's grandma) did too. So, what hope have I got?!

I will admit I've had hard times myself, but I've never been at the point where I've considered doing anything I can't come back from. It terrifies me that I could end up there, which motivates me to keep myself on a more even kilter, and come out of the darkness.

But I don't just want to be balancing on the edge of the darkness all the time. My default settings are anger, pain and sadness – but I'm working on changing that. I want to actually sit in the sunshine. I want to really feel all the beauty of life. I know I've said throughout this book that comfort zones and consistency are boring, but there's one thing that I would love to be boring and consistent, and that's my mental health. I would love for my mental state to feel stable. I don't know if that's possible, but I think it's something everyone should strive towards.

That's not to say I'm aiming to be happy every moment of every day. I think there's a real culture of toxic positivity at the moment, where the end-goal is just unadulterated happiness. I think it's dangerous to believe in that, because it's impossible to maintain that level of joy and comfort. The higher up you go . . . fuck me, that's a long way to fall to the bottom. When everything is great in your life, a bad time can hit you even harder.

Understandably, everyone wants to get rid of the sadness. They want life to be all rainbows, daisies and fucking bunnies. I really wish it was – I love rabbits. It pains me to see people striving for something they're never going to achieve, because then they'll always be disappointed. But also, I think there's a lot that can be gained from the harder moments of life. If you had never seen bad shit, then you wouldn't recognise good shit when it slaps you across the face.

Obviously, I wish I never had to see my mum like that when I was so young. But I think witnessing it has also made me who

I am. I think that seeing intense emotions in other people has made me more emotionally intelligent, and more able to read a situation. It has made me fiercely protective of the people I love, which I'd say is mostly a good quality. I also find it a lot easier to forgive people, because I know that even the best people go through the worst times and sometimes act without logic or reason. I know that emotions can do extreme things to people, which means they react in unpredictable ways. I think it has given me more empathy. What do you think your own traumas have taught you? I think you can find silver linings in even the biggest shit.

So how can we accept the shittier parts of life? I don't think there's one specific answer. It's not an easy thing to do. But I think it's about using those horrendous moments as fuel to move forward. You can look back at all the different things you have felt and gone through in your life, and say: 'That was fucking rough, but I came out the other side.' You've proven to yourself that it's possible to come out the other end. On your worst days, you made it through. You found the light eventually, no matter how dark that tunnel seemed at the time. The phrase 'this too shall pass' is so overused and, if you saw it come up on an Instagram post, you might just scroll past. It's hard for us to hear these kinds of phrases when we're in a hole, but they're so true. Everything passes. You only have to look at your past to remind you of that. You've been through so much crap, and yet you're still here. You're still trying. You're still looking for all of life's beautiful moments. You still have hope for better days. Of course, I'd do anything to take all the pain away, but we're human and we can't exist without pain. The hardest moments in life give us something to overcome and something to be proud of. Looking back at the past reminds us of our resilience and how far we've come.

If you love someone who is struggling with mental health issues, there's a tendency to want to solve the problem and fix them. I know we've spoken about this a few times already – when you love someone, all you want to do is take their pain away. That's a natural response. However, you need to accept that you can't. All you can do is be there, to listen. My nan was so good at that. She had a presence that made me (and my mum, and basically everyone she met) always feel like we were in a safe space with her. That's all we can do for the people we love: give them a safe space of support, especially when it feels unsafe for them in their own brains.

When we try to fix people, we sometimes end up making it worse. We pile on the pressure, panic them, and we let their problems and struggles overwhelm us. The best thing you can do to support someone else through a hard time is to focus on your own mental stability. The more stable you can be, the more you can act like a stone pillar for someone who is off-kilter. If you're flopping all over the place, you're not going to be a very good support, are you?

Ever since I was a kid, I've understood that it's important to hold myself together in order to be strong for other people. I haven't necessarily done that in the right way though. I've thought it was about telling everyone I'm strong – about faking it until I make it, basically. Since Nan died, I've reflected a lot and I know this isn't the right way of doing things. I always thought I didn't have the right to be upset or traumatised by what happened to Mum, because it was her pain. I can admit now that it was my pain too. Since Nan died, I've found it harder to put up that front and pretend I have everything together. Strengthening your mental health is an inside job. It's not something you can just project outwards. You have to do all the stuff I've spoken about in earlier chapters: find your 'thing' that makes you feel good, surround yourself with the right people and prioritise your mental health, before it has the chance to get bad. There are so many ways to do this and I'm not going to preach which approach is the best. You find your own. And remember, it ain't selfish to do so.

Even though I don't blame my mum anymore for what happened, I'm still working on removing the blame I have for myself. When I think about it too hard, I think: why didn't you stay downstairs, you fucking idiot? But I know that if someone else told me this same story and they were beating themselves up about it, I'd be so upset to hear that. It's painful to think about a kid blaming themselves for anything. I was twelve years old. I didn't know better. That wasn't a choice I had and it wasn't a mistake I made.

I think it's helpful to ask yourself those questions as if you're asking a friend, because it reveals your own ridiculous contradictions. From there, you can remind yourself: don't I deserve the same grace and respect that I give other people? You might have to remind yourself of this a million times. You can have a little breakthrough, and then you'll forget again. It's just repetition, ain't it? We have to train ourselves the same way we train dogs. You keep trying and trying until it becomes routine. If you keep saying, 'It wasn't my fault. I was only a child,' eventually you'll believe it. And when I say 'you', I mean 'me'.

I'm not in a position to offer advice on dealing with severe mental health problems. I'm not qualified. But what I would say is: if you're feeling terrible, tell someone. Speak to someone you trust or call a mental health helpline like CALM (0800 585858), Mind (0300 102 1234) or Samaritans (116 123). You might not feel like life is worth living right now, but things can change for the better. You just have to hold on.

My mum is living proof of that. Despite the fear I felt on that rainy, drunken night, I trust her more than I ever have. She has worked so hard on understanding herself better – probably harder than I have ever worked on myself. She has so much determination to make life better for herself and to live with her head held high. The darkness still creeps up occasionally, but she can recognise it and she knows when to reach out. When I told her I was going to write this book, she gave her blessing for me to talk about her mental health. I know it isn't easy for her to do, but I admire how open she is, because she knows that the more we can talk about this stuff, the easier it'll be for everyone else who is suffering. We live in such a connected world – we're all speaking to each other, all the time – but that doesn't mean it can't be lonely. If anything, it can be lonelier, because Instagram comments aren't quality connections. We think there's no one else in the world who will understand how we feel. And no one will fully understand, because we're all so unique. But even just connecting on one tiny thing can make the world of difference.

Me and Mum are both at a stage now where we're trying our best to be strong – genuinely strong, not just the illusion of strong – for each other. Nan was that person for both of us, so now we're trying to fill in the gaps and be that for each other. Just because someone has contemplated taking their own life, doesn't mean you can't rely on them. If anything, I feel like I can rely on her more. Mum might not have won the war, but she wins battles with her demons every single day. She's a fighter who is covered in scars. I can't think of anything stronger or more heroic than that.

Final Fucking Thoughts: You've got through the worst shit before. You can do it again

★ It's normal to have bad feelings about yourself every once in a while, but you just want enough good feelings that you can override the shit ones.

★ If you had never seen bad shit, then you wouldn't recognise good shit if it slapped you across the face.

★ The hardest moments in life give us something to overcome and something to be proud of. You can find silver linings in even the biggest shit.

CHAPTER 10

Learning to Live

So, there you have it. Now you've learned a lot more about the person behind the sarcastic jokes, receding hairline and head-to-toe tattoos. To be honest, I've learned a lot myself during this process too. Here's what I've discovered . . .

I'm a massive overthinker. It's strange, because this is not a word I would've used to describe myself. I normally describe Sam as an overthinker and I'm usually the voice of reason who will say, 'Mate, stop going around in circles, it's all good.' I'd like to describe myself as rational and logical. I make quick decisions and don't like to dwell on things. However, I overthink in a different way. I'm constantly thinking about the future and what's coming next, which means I find it hard to live in the present. I beat myself up and don't allow myself to enjoy good things because I'll be like, 'Yeah that's great, but you're still a shit person.' I have quite a 'fuck it' attitude that seems at odds with thinking too much, but I've realised both of these things are true. I'm a huge contradiction – and I'm pretty sure we all are.

I'm more scared than I thought I was. Again, if anyone ever called me a coward, I'd tell them to 'fuck off'. I've jumped out of planes. I've got my bollocks out on stage. One of the things on my bucket list is to scuba-dive with great white sharks. Nothing scares me! I'm 'Pirate Pete'! But, I'm not really. I don't shy away from confronting things that most people would find terrifying, yet I hide as much as I can from confronting myself. I'm scared of the future and what I'll think when I look back on my life. I'm scared of being happy. I'm scared of being in love. I'm scared of being close to people. And so, I take the easy way out. I remove myself from situations. I didn't think I was the kind of person to quit things, but really I'm an expert at running away. Or at least, I have been up until now. This is my starting line, but it's up to me how I want to finish.

I'm a perfectionist, but not in the way I thought I was. I've always known that I'm a control freak and I like things to be done well. But perfectionism is a good thing, right? It's about striving for the best and producing excellence. I'm always happy to try new things, even if I'm shit at them – I'm not put off by failure or rejection when it comes to work or activities, because I know I can keep trying and I'll get there in the end. However, the true meaning of perfectionism is needing things to be perfect to the extent that you don't even bother trying. I'm a perfectionist when it comes to anything emotional. It's why I struggle with relationships. For most things, I find knockbacks motivating. They make me want to be better. But emotionally, I hold myself to a different standard. I think I have to be perfect; otherwise, what's the point? I don't like to sit in emotional grey areas. I know a lot of that comes from me and a lot comes from how men are trained to respond to our emotions (basically: push them away). I'm learning that it's okay to be emotionally imperfect. It's okay to not always be strong. It's okay to be working through shit and to allow other people to see your flaws. I plan to keep repeating that to myself until I believe it.

I'm a selfish prick – but, again, not in the way you might think. I would've described my selfishness a bit like this: I like my own space, I do what I want, I don't give a fuck what anyone else thinks. These statements aren't entirely true. I do love being on my own, but I also want someone to share life's experiences with. I do what I want, but I would always avoid doing something that would hurt someone I care about. And I do give a fuck what the people who care about me think – specifically my mum and my friends. If anything, I ignore my issues and prefer to focus on other people. However, what does make me a selfish prick is the fact I turn inwards when I'm struggling. I think I know best, that I can handle things on my own, and I find it hard to let other people support and help me. It's actually quite a selfish trait: not allowing other people to love you. We all want to be loved, but we also want to give love. Denying someone the 'giving' part is actually fucking selfish. I hadn't thought about it like that before.

I blame and shame myself constantly – and that ain't right. Some of the shit that has happened in my life was 100 per cent my fault, don't get me wrong. There have been hundreds of times I've acted like a prick and really regret it. However, not everything was my fault. Some things happened *to* me and not *because* of me. It wasn't my fault that my parents split up. It isn't my fault that my mum has struggled with her mental health her whole life. And some things are only partly my fault: my tendency to feel angry or repress my emotions comes from my upbringing and how I have been socialised as a man. It's difficult for me to admit that, because it comes back to my control-freak tendencies. I want to feel like I'm in control of everything. The reality is, I'm not. None of us are. Only a small fraction of our lives are within our control. The important thing is to grab those parts by the balls and do the absolute best we can with what we've got.

It's weird, ain't it? I've only uncovered this stuff about myself at the age of thirty-five, after writing a whole book about myself. We spend so much time with ourselves every day (literally every waking moment), but we rarely interrogate who we actually are. We stay in the same patterns, in the same thought processes, in the same fucked-up beliefs. We rarely say: 'Hang on a minute, what am I doing? Why am I like this? Is there something I can be doing differently?' It's helpful to reflect on all this stuff, because you can't know where you're going until you know where you've been.

I know all those lessons sound negative, but I don't see it that way at all. It's a really positive thing to know what I'm working with. All of these things make me the person I am. Trust me, I know that the process of being honest with yourself can be confronting. It ain't nice to go: 'Oh, I'm an overthinking, selfish, perfectionist coward. Fantastic.' However, negative qualities all have flip sides too. I still find it hard to praise myself, but I can also say this: I work hard. I'm self-aware (or at least, I am more now). I care about things. My heart is in the right place, even if

I don't always make the right decisions. I am who I am – I know there's a lot about myself that I can't control or change. However, there's a lot that I *can* change and I won't stop trying to be a better version of myself.

There are some things I believed before I started this book that I now feel even more sure of . . .

Life is totally fucked. We lose people, we fall out with people and break up with people, we experience failure, we get fired, we get sick, we feel pain. However, there's so much that makes life beautiful, and it's possible to put a magnifying glass to those moments, rather than letting them dissolve into a huge pile of shit. There's the fact we have seemingly infinite room in our hearts to meet new people and love new people. Obviously I've never had kids, so I wouldn't know what that feels like, but I'm constantly picking up new mates and forming new connections as I get older, which is fucking beautiful. Just because you don't have connections you're happy about right now, doesn't mean you won't. You could meet someone every single day who could change your life. Then there's the fact dogs exist. Literally, how can you be sad around a dog? There's the fact most of you know me because you've watched reality TV shows or listened to me talk rubbish on a podcast for hours – I mean, isn't that fun? You get to just sit back and enjoy things every once in a while, have a laugh, be a bit silly. I still don't understand why you'd want to watch or listen to me, but I'm glad you get to have those moments regardless. We all need these moments, and they're all valuable.

Eternal happiness ain't possible – as much as I wish it was. You might be finally sitting down with your cuppa after tidying the whole house to read a book by some washed-up reality star, and then the phone will ring and you'll need to go help your nan who has fallen down the stairs. You can't wait for all the conditions of life to be absolutely perfect before you decide to enjoy it, because anything can happen at any time. Perfection doesn't exist. Forget the lies you've been fed on social media; ignore the 'a picture speaks a thousand words' bollocks. Pictures only speak a few words. The full story behind a picture is silent and you'll probably never hear it. It's a waste of time comparing your whole life to other people's highlight reels. Your time would be better spent doing literally anything else. Just because you don't have your 'perfect' body yet, you can still go on holiday. Just because you're not the best singer, doesn't mean you can't get up on stage at the karaoke bar. Don't wait around to enjoy your life. Do it right now.

We're all a bit broken. Every single one of us has problems. Denying that ain't going to get you anywhere. We all have things we've done that we wish we hadn't. We've all had things happen to us when we wish they didn't. But that doesn't make us any less beautiful. It's like if you looked at a massive statue that was meticulously crafted by some artist bloke thousands of years ago. It probably has a few cracks in it, and it's covered in bird shit. But that doesn't make it any less beautiful, does it? The statue was only ever perfect the moment it was created, and then it went downhill from there. That's the same as us. We're perfect when we're born and then we go downhill, as all that life experience accumulates like cracks and bird shit. Still, you're no less important than the day you were born. You can fix those cracks and clean the shit, but new ones will come. I know this analogy is going on forever, but you get what I'm trying to say. You might be a little messed up here and there, but you can keep on making yourself better. You're still worth something.

Your life's journey is yours, and yours alone. I know I've been self-indulgently talking about my life the whole way through this book, and I know some of my stories might feel completely disconnected from your own reality. It makes sense, because we are all so unique. We've all had completely differ-ent upbringings and experiences, and we all have unique thoughts running through our brains. It might feel lonely to admit that, but actually it's a strength. It's your superpower that there's not one other person in the world who is exactly like you. Acknowledging that means you can learn to live your life in the most authentic way possible. You can tune into what you really want and block out all the other shit that says you 'should' be doing or being something different. There's nothing wrong with you if other people's advice hasn't worked for you (even mine). It's your own journey, and you have to find your own way. This understanding can also help you remember that we are all the main characters in our own stories. The people around you don't exist as your supporting actors. Likewise, you can't fix or solve other people's problems, as much as you can do your best to support them. They have to go on their own adventure. The only person you can have full responsibility over is yourself.

Acceptance is a very important skill to have. I'm not so good at this one, but I'm striving to be better. The more you can accept the shittier parts of life, the better equipped you'll be to enjoy all the good parts. It's all about expectations, ain't it? If you think you can cure your mental health and solve all your problems (and other people's), you'll feel constantly disappointed. Accept your flaws. Accept your past. Accept the fact people will piss you off, most days. Accept that there will always, always be terrible traffic on your commute. I'm not saying you should give up on trying to make things better, I just think you should take the pressure off yourself and the pursuit of perfection. Acceptance is the first step towards genuine contentment. And how do you work on becoming more accepting? That part, I'm still figuring out.

Nothing will ever be enough. You'll never make enough money. There will never be enough parties to go to or flashy watches to buy. You won't have enough hours in the day to do all the things you want to do. You'll never be the best at anything – there will always be someone who is better. We live in a world of more, more, more . . . and nothing in life is ever enough. However, my perspective on that phrase has changed. It's all about acceptance and embracing imperfection, while still striving to be the best version of yourself. Nothing will ever be enough, but that's okay. It's your job to look within yourself, to find what is enough for you. It's your job to look within yourself to discover that you *are* enough, exactly as you are.

I'm not a fan of self-help books, and I never wanted this to be one of those; although, now I think that maybe I did write my own personal self-help book. I've realised I have all the tools I need within myself to make the changes that can make my life better. I know that I can accept my life; I can accept myself and feel proud for going on this journey. I know where I've been, where I am and where I want to be. I want to appreciate all the (many, many) blessings in my life. I want to prove to my nan that I *can* find comfort in happiness.

I hope you've gained something from reading my book, but I think now it's time for you to go away and write your own self-help book. You also have all the tools you need to move forward – you just have to look hard enough to find them. So go on then, off you fuck. Ta-ra.

Useful Organisations

Campaign Against Living Miserably (CALM)
www.thecalmzone.net • 0800 585858

Frank
www.talktofrank.com • 0300 1236600

Mental Health Foundation
www.mentalhealth.org.uk

Mind
www.mind.org.uk • 0300 102 1234

Samaritans
www.samaritans.org • 116 123

SANE
www.sane.org.uk • 0300 304 7000

Acknowledgements

Nan,

I know you never thought I'd actually talk about how I feel with anyone but you . . . but I'm trying. This book, despite not being something I wanted to do, has helped me. It's helped me remember you with a smile and not just an overwhelming feeling of loss and pain.

I would give anything to have you here and no words will ever be enough to describe the impact you had on my life – you were my best friend and my soul mate. The only good parts of me came from you and despite my many fuck ups, I hope one day when I look back, I can feel as if I made you proud.

I miss you.

Mum,

I know reading this book will hurt and there are many things we have never spoken about, but the most important thing to me is that you know how much I love you and how much I admire you every day. You are the strongest person I know, and no one is prouder than I am when I see how far you've come. The inspiration behind this book is you, the bravery you have, facing every day – the way you do this is inspiring. Your story is special, you are special.

I'm sorry I didn't understand your pain and I'm sorry that I couldn't have done more, but know I will always be here, I will always love you.

Thank you for showing me unconditional love and supporting me no matter what. I am blessed to have you as my mum and you truly are my fucking hero.

I love you.

Mokkingbird Dream Team
It's been a decade… I couldn't think of a better team to share this weird and fucking wonderful journey with. Thank you for always having my back, personally and professionally. You are not just my management, more importantly, you are my friends.

Arielle (my favourite Swiftie)
Thank you for your patience, thank you for your understanding, and thank you for becoming a true friend… but please stop sending me fucking Taylor Swift lyrics.

To my publishing team – Jo at Bell Lomax Moreton and the amazing Lauren and the team at Catalyst and Hodder – thanks for the opportunity. You've been a dream team and I am so grateful. I know I haven't made its easy, but I appreciate you so much.

Picture Acknowledgements

Page numbers refer to pages within the plate sections.

Pages 1–5 and page 10: All courtesy of the Author's family.

Additional sources:
Shutterstock: page 6/Beretta/Sims, page 8 below/Ken McKay/
ITV, page 9 centre right/ITV/Nicky Johnston, page 9 below/Ken
McKay/ITV, page 14 above, page 14 centre and below/ITV.
© James Rudland: page 7, page 13 above.
© Shine TV Limited/The Natural Studios: page 8 above left
and above right.
Matt Monfredi: page 9 above.
© Lime Pictures Ltd: page 11 above.
© UKTV/Adam Lawrence: page 11 below.
Shine TV Limited/Ziji Productions: page 12 above.
Vivienne Edge Photography/@vivienneedgephotography: page
13 below left and below right.
Courtesy of CoppaFeel! (Marco Barcella): page 15.
Pete Dadds: page 16.